The
Milkshake
Moment

The
Milkshake
Moment

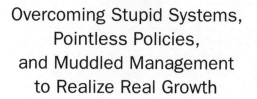

Overcoming Stupid Systems,
Pointless Policies,
and Muddled Management
to Realize Real Growth

STEVEN S. LITTLE

WILEY

John Wiley & Sons, Inc.

Published by John Wiley & Sons, Inc., Hoboken, New Jersey.
Published simultaneously in Canada.

For general information on our other products and services or for technical support, please contact our Customer Care Department within the United States at (800) 762-2974, outside the United States at (317) 572-3993 or fax (317) 572-4002.

Wiley also publishes its books in a variety of electronic formats. Some content that appears in print may not be available in electronic books. For more information about Wiley products, visit our web site at www.wiley.com.

ISBN 978-0-470-25746-3

Printed in the United States of America

10 9 8 7 6 5 4 3 2 1

To Tyler,
for making us all so proud.

Contents

Contents

Acknowledgments

First, I need to thank everyone who is included in this book. Whether you are a client, an acquaintance, a hero, a friend or a family member, I sincerely appreciate you letting me tell others about your Milkshake Moments.

I also owe a great debt of gratitude to the entire 2007 Pow-Wow Posse. Jane Atkinson (who is indispensable), Todd Sattersten (who is thoughtful), Tom Ryan (who is hilarious), Dan Heath (who is clever), Lora Plauche (who is unique), and Barbara Cave Hendricks (who is inspiring) all helped me learn to finally embrace my inner milkshake. Tim Leffel was also in the Nashville tee-pee and continued to be my daily sounding board and heavy-lifter for this entire project. If patience is a virtue, Tim Leffel is destined for sainthood. Muchas gracias to his wife and daughter for sharing their hubby and daddy again this year.

Speaking of saints, Violet Cieri is the Marketing Maven, heart, soul, and tireless voice-of-reason for the entire "Steve the Speecher" team. Nothing, including this book, would be possible without her persistence and professionalism. The fact that she is also a true friend is like a dollop of whipped cream. Her laughter is the cherry on top. Ashley Novasad is also a friend and colleague who becomes my Wilmington eyes, ears, and, most recently, even nose. Please don't leave us Ashley . . . who else is going to listen to my "Jiggly Wiggly" stories? TinaMarie Goesswein keeps us all organized with a smile.

I am in great debt to my editor and amigo Matt Holt and all the other great folks at Wiley such as Miriam Palmer-Sherman and Kim Dayman. Matt, I really appreciate your ability to see with my point-of-view every now and again. I know it can be a chore. Shannon Vargo went well beyond the call of duty. Her edits have significantly improved this book.

Sister Jenny, mother of the incredible Fletcher, was an early rough draft reader who helped me whittle away the superfluous. Mother Susan, daughter of the legendary Tom, provided much of the Paw-Paw details.

My new friend Joanne Berk also contributed immensely to this final product, with both a keen eye for continuity and a thorough understanding of why Milkshake Moments should matter. Thanks for working on such a tight time crunch Joanne. See you in Seattle.

Finally, I would like to express immense gratitude to Lora, Alaina, GG and Tyler for helping me see "everything," even when the dreaded deadlines clouded my vision. Like Violet says, I am now officially the luckiest man in the world. Sooner!

Section 1
The Milkshake Moment

Chapter 1

It Was a Dark and Stormy Night

The story you're about to read is true. Of course everything you will read in this book is true, but this story is particularly true because it happened to me. A few years ago I traveled to Baltimore, Maryland, for a speaking engagement.

Anyone who travels for business knows that it is hardly glamorous. After 9/11, however, it became even more frustrating, and it keeps getting worse. I don't think I'd be overstating it to say that business travel today is horrific: irretrievably lost luggage, annoying security searches, perpetually oversold flights, infuriating rental car policies, frazzled counter staff . . . I think you get the picture.

Despite all the traumas of travel, I decided a few years ago to always keep a smile on my face. The way I look at it: if the business travel industry gets the best of me, they win and I lose. I just can't allow that to happen.

I keep a smile on my face by keeping my eye on a prize. My prize at the end of every business travel day is a vanilla milkshake . . . a thick, gooey, luscious, indulgent vanilla milkshake. I'm talking a hand-dipped, old-fashioned, malt-shoppy kind of milkshake. I don't just like 'em; I *love* 'em. Both my career and my mental well-being literally depend on them. The image of that milkshake is the proverbial dangling carrot that gets me through even the worst travel day.

It had been a particularly difficult day of planes, trains, and automobiles. I was to arrive at the Baltimore/ Washington International (BWI) Airport at 7:00 P.M. for dinner with my clients at 8:00 P.M. Unfortunately, I arrived at midnight. In other words, there was nothing out of the ordinary so far.

I grabbed my bags and stood in a long taxicab line to take the 20-minute ride to Baltimore's beautiful Inner Harbor. I was cold, wet, tired, and hungry, but smiling, because I was going to get that vanilla milkshake. Pulling up to the hotel at this late hour, the thought occurred to me, "At least there won't be a long line to check in." But once inside I realized I wasn't the only one having a difficult travel day. Apparently the entire Eastern seaboard was similarly inconvenienced, and it appeared most of those travelers were also staying at my hotel. I faced a 30-minute wait just to check in. *Keep your eye on the prize, Steve . . . keep your eye on the prize.*

4

The thought of that milkshake was still working its magic. I could almost taste it. Everyone else in the lobby must have been wondering why I was smiling.

Eventually it was my turn and I was given one of those plastic magnetic keys for room #809. I put one bag on each shoulder, trudged over to the elevator banks, pushed the button for the eighth floor, and found my room. After deciphering the electronic door handle schematic, I repeatedly swiped my plastic key—but to no avail. It didn't work. The room remained locked. So close, yet so far.

As any business traveler knows, getting a plastic key that actually works is always an iffy proposition at best. In my own personal experience, the incidence of hotel key failure is directly proportional to the cumulative road hassles of that given day. Rehoisting my bags, I shuffled back down to the lobby.

Keep your eye on the prize, Steve . . . keep your eye on the prize. See your milkshake. Be your milkshake.

I returned to the front desk and got in line with the other people holding faulty room keys. I was still the only one smiling.

I returned to room #809 with my second key and this time it worked. *Yes!* I didn't even put the bags down.

It Was a Dark and Stormy Night

I hurried straight to the phone and immediately hit the button for room service. As soon as I heard the ring on the other end, my mouth began to water. The moment had arrived. It was time to claim my prize.

"Good evening, Mr. Little, this is Stuart in room service. How may I help you?" Stuart's voice brimmed with enthusiasm. He was so chipper, filled with the idealism of youth. *Quite the eager beaver for one o'clock in the morning.* Yet he sounded quite polite and well trained. At this point in the transaction, I was relatively encouraged . . . at this point, anyway.

"Stuart, I'd like a vanilla milkshake, please," I said. A seemingly simple request, right? Well, not quite.

"I'm sorry, Mr. Little, but we don't have milkshakes," Stuart replied regretfully.

I was crushed. In that instant, my smile flickered. Quickly I regrouped.

"All right, Stuart, let me ask you this: Do you have any vanilla ice cream?"

"Yes, of course!" he responded with renewed enthusiasm.

"Okay, Stuart, I'd like a full bowl of vanilla ice cream."

6

The Milkshake Moment

"Yes sir, right away, sir! Is there anything else I can do to serve you?" Stuart asked.

"Yeah . . . do you have any milk?"

"Yes, we have milk!" he replied confidently.

"All right, Stuart, here's what I would like you to do. Please send up a tray with a full bowl of vanilla ice cream, half a glass of milk, and a long spoon. Could you do that for me, please?"

"Certainly, right away, sir," Stuart responded triumphantly.

I hung up the phone and a few minutes later there was a knock. Sure enough, at my door there was a tray with a full bowl of vanilla ice cream, half a glass of milk, and a long spoon—everything needed to make a vanilla milkshake. But of course they didn't have vanilla milkshakes.

Now let me ask you an important question. Is Stuart stupid?

Chapter 2

Half Empty or Half Full?

Seriously, is Stuart stupid? It's a legitimate question. Certainly an argument could be made for Stuart's stupidity.

However, for all I knew, Stuart could just as easily have been a certified genius. After all, he did manage to pull together precisely what I ordered, down to the half glass of milk (a somewhat unusual request).

Frankly, Stuart's IQ is beside the point. For the purposes of this book, let's assume Stuart is not stupid. It's the system that's stupid.

Stuart's behavior is not unique. Like the vast majority of employees everywhere, Stuart wanted to do a good job. To this day, he probably still thinks he did.

In Chapter 1 I promised to tell you the full truth, and here it is: out of the 100 or so hotel rooms I stay in every year, I run this experiment approximately half the time. It's not every night, as some hotels don't offer room service, while others specifically offer milkshakes. I conduct

9

this experiment only when a milkshake is not on the room service menu. More often than not, they *do* have all the ingredients to make me happy. Yet I usually end up with the same full bowl of ice cream, half a glass of milk, and a long spoon (some assembly required).

Why does this keep happening? Why can't individuals like Stuart deliver Milkshake Moments? I've had plenty of time to ponder that question now that I've received over 200 do-it-yourself vanilla milkshakes from America's leading business hotels. Let's take a look at some of the underlying causes that lead to these systemic breakdowns.

Stuart is standing at a point-of-sale screen popping in orders with his company-issued plastic access key. For all intents and purposes, his key is as dysfunctional as my original room key. If his screen doesn't say "milkshake," then a milkshake simply does not exist, and the most magical key in the world can't make one appear. The supposedly foolproof system is designed to ensure that Stuart can't make the organization appear foolish. Yet even a casual observer can see that the system has pushed the organization well beyond foolish. It is now sitting squarely in the land of lost opportunity. How's that for irony?

Think about this. I represent the mother lode for the business travel industry. Remember, I stay in over 100 hotel rooms a year and I'm not exactly price sensitive.

Stuart could have charged me $25 for that milkshake and I would have been happy to pay it.

I actually feel sorry for the major business hotel chains. In an effort to standardize their systems, they've taken individual judgment out of the equation. They spend billions of dollars in marketing to get people like me through their doors and billions more in staff training to make my kind happy. Yet they continually blow it, due in some part to a stupid point-of-sale system. But that's just the tip of the proverbial iceberg. It goes much deeper than that.

Let me ask you this: Do you think there was a blender in the kitchen? No, it was in the bar. And as anyone who has ever worked in the hospitality industry knows, the bar staff and the kitchen staff don't always play nicely together. For them, sharing is often a challenge. I want "food and beverage," and they're offering me "food" and "beverage." They're like the Hatfields and McCoys, two warring factions that have been doing battle for so long they have forgotten what they're fighting about. In fact, many times they're not even working for the hotel: The two functions have been outsourced to competing organizations. Now, that's a stupid system.

Legend has it that Stuart arrived on the front lines at the height of the Great Blender Wars of 2004. He got caught in the crossfire and is still a little skittish about

Half Empty or Half Full?

approaching enemy lines. Maybe his commanding officer warned him to avoid the minefield of "special orders." Undoubtedly, his trenchmates have convinced him that keeping his head down is the only way to survive.

Any time there is a breakdown like this, the root causes go well beyond the obvious limitations of a third-party point-of-sale system or the internal politics of blender access. Despite my feelings to the contrary that fateful night, Stuart's inability to deliver a Milkshake Moment is not the end of the world. It is, however, symptomatic of a much broader organizational malaise.

This milkshake story is not just another example of bad customer service. It's much more than that. This is a larger tale of lost opportunity. Invariably, the root cause can be traced back to factors that are much more fundamental. Peel back the bureaucratic layers of any organization and you will find a broad range of self-imposed limitations, from antiquated hiring practices to poor workspace design to short-term financial myopia.

Here's another way to look at it.

Imagine, if you will, a championship football game that has come down to its final seconds. Your team, behind by two points, has managed to move the ball into field goal range. With the clock stopped, out trots your team's rookie field goal kicker, Shanky Wydewright.

A hush falls upon the 80,000 in attendance as millions more watch anxiously at home. The moment of truth has arrived. Everything hinges on this one kick. If Shanky makes it, your team scores three points and walks away with the championship trophy. If he misses it, your season comes to a sudden and heartbreaking end. *Come on, Shanky! Shan-ky! Shan-ky!*

Be he hero or goat, the headlines the following day will pin the victory or defeat on the narrow shoulders of Shanky Wydewright ("Wydewright Delivers Delight" or "Fans Cranky Over Bungling Shanky").

Like Stuart, our kicker Shanky is just the visible manifestation of a much larger organizational undertaking. Any coach will tell you that winning or losing a game is about much more than a single kick. An infinite number of variables leads a team to this moment.

How well did they draft offensive linemen four years ago? Did the newly hired strength training coach make a difference in this year's team stamina? Did two second-quarter penalties keep your team from having a larger halftime lead? How many season tickets did the front office sell? Did increased attendance lead to increased enthusiasm? Did that increased enthusiasm subsequently contribute to one extra victory in the regular season, thereby guaranteeing home field advantage in the playoffs? Did home field advantage ensure that you're playing inside a dome in December, taking weather conditions out of Shanky's equation?

In either instance, be it Shanky or Stuart, the outcome largely depends on position. For Shanky, if the team can get the ball down to the 15-yard line, his success is pretty much a given. Put Shanky at midfield and his chances of splitting the uprights are very unlikely. In Stuart's case, organizational shackles keep him out of position. He is so far removed from the organizational purpose that he can no longer see the ultimate goal. In order for an organization to truly succeed, the Stuarts of the world need to believe that they are in a position to deliver Milkshake Moments.

Consider your organization. When are you saying no when it would be much better and just as easy to say yes? Are you really putting people in the best position to grow? Do your current policies, procedures, and systems enable you to truly deliver?

So what is a Milkshake Moment? It's certainly not a full bowl of ice cream, half a glass of milk, and a long spoon. Instead, a Milkshake Moment is a brave individual action, be it big or small, that furthers the cause of growth in an organization. Milkshake Moments materialize when individuals understand the organization's true purpose, honestly believe it is their job to fulfill it, and are given the tools and the freedom to make it happen. When a would-be growth leader managing deep within the bowels of a stagnating organization has the guts to stand up and say, "This idea is contrary to everything we say we believe," that's a Milkshake Moment. When a thinking person is given the freedom to seize an opportunity afforded by change, that's a Milkshake Moment. When a small business owner consciously puts purpose before profit, that's a Milkshake Moment. When the executive director of a nonprofit foundation challenges the status quo views of her tenured board members, that's a Milkshake Moment.

This book is about that precise, critical point in time when members of twenty-first-century organizations realize they are allowed to do the right thing—to serve the interests of others in order to grow the organization—instead of following arcane, arbitrary rules, processes, and procedures that actually hinder growth. Only when we remove our own self-imposed barriers can we seize new opportunities in structured settings. A Milkshake Moment can only be realized when growth leaders clearly communicate an organization's true purpose and grant individuals permission to do whatever can be done ethically to achieve it.

Chapter 3

This Is *Not* a Customer Service Book

I know you're not stupid. How do I know? First of all, you're reading a book, which puts you ahead of most people. According to my publisher, only 20 percent of business books purchased are actually read. The rest of them just sit there looking impressive up on a bookshelf. I also know you're smart because you bought this particular book, which is a testament to your astute judgment.

And while your intellect may be superior to that of your nonreading peers, the vast majority of them aren't stupid, either. I know it may be hard to believe that assistant manager Bill Blowhard isn't intellectually challenged, but it's usually only his actions that are stupid. Sure, plenty of organizations have a dunce or two on the payroll. However, when most people behave stupidly in an organization, it usually has little to do with their innate intelligence. Somehow, organizations filled with relatively smart people do a whole lot of really stupid things.

17

The biggest obstacle to Milkshake Moments lies in the very nature of organizations and the systems they build and embrace. While supposedly setting their sights on innovative growth initiatives, they are continually shooting themselves in the foot. I work with a wide variety of organizations interested in growth: Fortune 500 companies, small closely held businesses, nonprofit fund-raisers, and local chambers of commerce. Invariably, they all gravitate at some point toward the same growth-stifling behaviors. To paraphrase cartoon strip character Pogo, "We have met the enemy and it is us."

(**A smart system can work with a little stupidity, but a stupid system can't work with even a lot of smarts.**)

So what does it take to break the cycle of stupidity and mix more milkshakes? In this book I discuss the five primary ingredients you need to make Milkshake Moments possible:

1. Foster "grow" versus status quo
2. Put purpose before profit
3. Solve the "people problem" problem
4. Insource crucial judgment
5. Care for customers

I also offer specific ways you can "mix it up" at the end of each chapter. You'll find a few "extra toppings" at the end of each section.

Breaking cycles starts with the deliberate actions of a dedicated growth leader. I'm assuming that's you. I don't know if you are a company president, a county commissioner, or a newly hired management trainee. What I do know is that growth is rarely accidental. Real growth occurs only when true leaders actually lead, clearing obstacles, illuminating weaknesses, championing changes, and seizing opportunities. If you want to grow, it is incumbent upon you to smash the obstacles to growth. If you want to be perceived as a true leader, start behaving like a cop on the stupidity beat.

I have met literally thousands of would-be growth leaders, and I can honestly tell you that most are merely managers. Their actions are small and incremental in nature, aimed at perpetuating the status quo. *Managers* and *growth* are rarely in the same meeting.

My first book was called *The 7 Irrefutable Rules of Small Business Growth* (John Wiley & Sons, 2005). It was written for the business owner looking to take his or her group to the next level. But upon its release, a funny thing began to happen. Big companies started to see that my rules applied to them as well. So did nonprofits and

This Is *Not* a Customer Service Book

faith-based institutions. They all helped me see that the issues surrounding growth are much the same across all organizations. Eventually, I came to understand that these rules can be applied across all human endeavors.

Of course not all organizations want to grow, but the ones that don't want to are the exceptions. Most are trying to grow something, on some level. Very few organizations are winding themselves down on purpose. I have yet to see a mission statement that seeks to maximize stakeholder dissatisfaction, thereby retarding revenue and moving closer to short-term irrelevance and long-term extinction.

In my first book I defined growth by top-line and bottom-line increases. That's how you keep score in the game called business. Naturally, growth can mean much more than increased sales or revenue. For a trade association, growth may be defined as increased membership or stronger legislative impact. For a charity, it could vary from enhanced awareness to greater donations for research. The common point is this: Real organizational growth isn't a project. It isn't the preferred outcome of a few ad hoc task force meetings. Real growth serves a worthy purpose beyond the mere perpetuation of the organization itself.

This book is about that precise moment, that critical instant in time, when twenty-first-century "organization person" realizes they are allowed to do the right thing, despite all evidence to the contrary.

Only when organizations get out of their own way can they achieve real, sustainable growth. Only when we remove our own self-imposed barriers can individuals seize new opportunities in an organizational setting.

In effect, this book is a call to arms. Regardless of who you are, what you do, or where you do it, it is up to you to be personally invested in your organization's growth. I regularly talk with "managers" who lament, "I agree with everything you said today, Steve. The problem isn't me—it's the idiots who work above/below/beside me that just don't get it." If after reading this book you are still certain that it is the other people in your organization who are truly hopeless, then you need to quit.

That's right. I mean you should literally quit doing what you're doing and go find a place where you can flourish. Life is way too short to waste your time and effort in a stagnating environment. I'm willing to bet you'll come to realize instead that it's not those around you who are the problem. It's actually the inherent nature of organizations that is your true nemesis. It takes guts to lead others away from the status quo. Growth requires persevering, creative, even courageous individuals who aren't afraid to mix it up.

21

Section 2
Foster "Grow" versus Status Quo

Why are so many organizations seemingly incapable of delivering Milkshake Moments?

For one, organizations tend to breed managers, not leaders. But managers are not what we need in these constantly changing times. Simply managing to meet the status quo will not help foster growth in the future. Sustainable growth requires the guidance of a true leader who looks to the future, grabs opportunities, and unleashes everyone's full potential.

Too often, managers within organizations keep making the same stupid mistakes. Like alcoholics following in the family footsteps, they tend to keep managing the same way they were managed, despite having firsthand evidence it doesn't really work. Most of their systems are set up to perpetuate existing processes, regardless of their effectiveness. People don't like change at all, and if they must change, then it becomes a manager's job to over think the transformation and make it even more complicated.

Why are we our own worst enemies? Why do even the most successful organizations manage to screw up regularly? Why is it so hard to get even the basics right in the organizations of today?

To find some answers, we've got to look at where we are and take a step back in time to see how we got here.

Chapter 4

A Brief History of Organizations and Man(agement)

Let's face it: On the whole, we're not very good at this thing we call "the organization." I'll be citing some prime examples of organizational shortcomings throughout this book, but you already know it's true without me even trying. We all know it. We see it all the time in our workplaces, schools, governments, softball leagues, and the like. Why are so many organizations so frustratingly ineffectual?

The best reason, I suppose, is that the concept itself is so new that we haven't had time to master it. While we are all certainly hardwired to be social beings, apparently our genetic code doesn't provide us a natural predisposition for building and maintaining complex hierarchies (as opposed to the instincts of bees and ants).

I don't know your religious beliefs, and I'm not here to step on them, but recently I heard an anthropologist speak at a business conference who said that most experts in the scientific community now believe that modern human beings, or Homo sapiens, have been roaming this planet for some 200,000 years, give or take a few millennia. (If your number is different, let's just agree we've been here a long time.) For the vast majority of our time on this planet we were hunter-gatherers, with no real need for organizations beyond the specific small, nomadic tribe we were trying to feed and protect.

Eventually, somebody wandering in the Fertile Crescent had a true Milkshake Moment and exclaimed, "Hey, everybody, we don't have to keep moving around all the time! This darn crescent is so darn fertile, we can grow and herd everything we need right here!" Thus was born the agricultural revolution, which just happened a mere 10,000 years ago. What were we thinking for the previous 190,000 years? I guess we weren't.

By some 6,000 years ago, we were getting so good at the agriculture thing we had time to build rudimentary hierarchies to help preserve it. New organizational institutions were created, including governments, religions, armies, and tax collectors. A couple thousand years later we saw the growth of the first true empires across the globe. Inevitably, these empires became bulky and inefficient. Like organizations today, they were pretty good at self-preservation, but they tended to stifle innovation. Milkshake Moments were few and far between.

The indomitable power of the individual prevailed, however, and eventually, two giant Milkshake Moments rescued us from these dark ages. The navigational compass gave us the ability to explore new places and then return safely home to tell others about them. The printing press came shortly thereafter. Shared wisdom led to the Renaissance, which led to the Age of Reason and the Enlightenment.

In 1776, wild-eyed revolutionaries like Thomas Jefferson and Ben Franklin shook up the world with one of history's most profound Milkshake Moments. Their declaration made the audacious claim that "all men are created equal." The philosophical debates that led to their fight for independence focused on the power of organizations—in this period usually governments—versus the rights of the individual.

The nineteenth century ushered in the need for an entirely new look at organizations. The Scientific method made mass production possible. To meet the needs of this industrial revolution, today's modern manager was created.

By the first half of the twentieth century, industrial-era organizations had difficulty discerning between man and machine. In the name of efficiency, detached managers often quashed the potential power of the individual. Mines got mined, railroads got built, and steel got forged, but often with a high human toll.

A Brief History of Organizations and Man(agement)

By the 1950s, bestsellers like *The Man in the Gray Flannel Suit* and *The Organization Man* suggested that all was not well in America's organizational hierarchies.

Academics also started to recognize the importance of the individual in organizational endeavors. Led by Peter Drucker, the father of modern management, business schools began to acknowledge that people weren't machines after all. Drucker had more than his fair share of Milkshake Moments while defining the role of the modern manager in an information age. He even came to dislike the terms *management* and *manager*, saying, "Most of what we call management consists of making it difficult for people to get their work done." In other words, Drucker believed that modern managers actually prevented Milkshake Moments from ever occurring.

The past 50 years of organizational thinking have seen a seemingly endless series of management trends and fads, most trying to resolve this inherent conflict: Organizations are focused on the perpetuation of the organization itself, whereas individuals are usually concerned with their own self-interest. This relatively new paradox creates tension between the forces of the organization and the will of the individual. Tension creates energy that can be used for both creation and destruction. Today, it is clear that any organization is made more powerful by harnessing the potential power of its individuals. By allowing individuals to create Milkshake Moments, growth leaders are putting everyone in a position to win.

So what's the point of this short history of (man)agement? It's simply this: It has taken us eons to get to this point, but we now know what works. We know which fundamental practices lead to organizational growth. We also know what doesn't work. There are plenty of organizations that know the difference, thereby realizing real growth. There simply should be more like them, and that is the point of *The Milkshake Moment*.

Remember, for 190,000 years we didn't have any organizations at all. The modern organization has been around for only a few hundred years. Indeed the very word *organization* itself didn't have today's definition in many English dictionaries until after World War II. If you consider the long history of people walking around on this planet, the type of organization we're familiar with is very, very young.

Mix It Up!

Approach the latest management fads and fashions cautiously. They often create more growth barriers than growth opportunities.

A Brief History of Organizations and Man(agement)

Chapter 5

Toddlers and Trust

If aliens came to visit our planet today, they might easily assume that toddlers are pretty stupid. Toddlers can't feed themselves well, have little in the way of spoken language skills, and exhibit a wanton disregard for sharp table corners. Indeed, they don't have the sense to avoid obvious environmental dangers such as hot stoves and big brothers. When provoked, they just sit on the floor and cry. Therefore, aliens could easily surmise that toddlers are inferior. But we know better.

Many businesses, government institutions, school systems, and associations are very much like toddlers, full of potential and promise. They are not inherently stupid; it's just that the concept of an organization is so new to this world that many are not able to fully fend for themselves. To reach their full potential, toddlers need true parenting, not just caretaking. Likewise, in order to grow, organizations need true leadership, not simply management. Individuals in organizations yearn for leaders they can trust and, in turn, follow.

In my first book I described the seven specific areas in which growth entrepreneurs should concentrate their time, money, and overall effort. It's within these seven areas that proven entrepreneurial leaders look to find the innovations and evolutions that foster sustained growth.

What I've come to learn is that growth leaders are distinctive not only in their actions, but also in their attributes. These specific attributes are more like personality traits than true management skills, and they ultimately build TRUST:

Timely
Realistic
Unscripted
Sensitive
Transparent

Timely—Every day I deal with people who say they want to grow their company, community, or association. And I know they truly mean it. Often one of the key factors that impede their progress, however, is how they choose to allocate their time and that of others. When I look at how they actually spend their time, I find that they revert back to their default setting—what they know best. They fill their days working on the tasks they are most comfortable completing.

In contrast, successful leaders devote the majority of their time to those areas that truly need it. They make timely decisions as often as decisions are needed—no more and no less.

Time is not something to be filled with activity for activity's sake. Leaders understand the nature of time and are skilled at prioritizing it to make an impact. They understand that being timely does not come from Day-Timers, longer hours, or an increasing workload. For some, this prowess is innate. For others it is a skill that must be honed through experience. Yet make no mistake about it; it is impossible to lead a growth charge without mastering the importance of time.

(Most managers simply get up and do what they want to do. Growth leaders get up and do what needs to be done.)

Realistic—Many joke that reality is overrated. It certainly is easier to don our rose-colored glasses and see only what we want to see. What distinguishes growth leaders is their unrelenting focus on what really is and what truly can be. While positive thinking has its place, delusions are dangerous.

"Our product is the best." "Our team is superior." "Our customers love us." "Our cause is more important than any other." *Really?* Let's can the empty slogans, take down

33

the banners, and throw away the T-shirts. Today, it takes a pragmatic realist to separate the true picture from the conventional groupthink.

Facing reality isn't merely a good idea; it's an imperative. Your organization is depending on someone to challenge the organization's most closely held beliefs today. Why couldn't that be a leader like you? Too often, closely held beliefs are kept on our shelves long past their expiration dates. Growth leaders seek only the truth and welcome any and all reality checks.

Unscripted—Today our world is filled with skeptics. People are simply jaded, and why shouldn't they be? Over the past 50 years we've lived through disgraced presidents, dubious armed conflicts, pilfered pensions, and "new and improved" products that are clearly neither new nor improved. We live in a world where much of what comes at us from organizations is spin, propaganda, and distorted half-truths. It should be obvious to any twenty-first-century leader that many people are reluctant to believe anything. Everyone's bullshit detector has become finely calibrated.

What we long for is authenticity. We want leaders who speak plainly and from the heart, not from talking points. We want bosses who reject corporate mumbo jumbo. We want professionals who don't cloak themselves in a blanket of CYA-speak.

In order to lead, it is critical to master the art of authenticity. Reject the tired clichés, lose the latest buzzwords, and say what you mean and mean what you say.

Sensitive—This is a loaded term. While it has many definitions, here I mean perceptive. Sensitive leaders are acutely aware of their surroundings and are keenly observant. They have an intuitive knack for understanding the motivations of others. They are able to feel the barely perceptible winds of change long before the actual storm. They have the uncanny ability to gain insight from seemingly disparate data.

How well do you read others in complex social situations? How much do you trust your gut feelings? How well do you handle displays of emotion in yourself and others? How easily do you move from perception to action?

Most growth leaders are naturals at these types of skills. Others need to regularly extricate themselves from day-to-day activities to work on them. Either way, being sensitive is an attribute that gives leaders another arrow in their organizational growth quiver.

Transparent—It's human nature not to trust those who attempt to hide things from us. For instance, when an organization gets into trouble and spirals downward because of a public relations crisis, it nearly always has

Toddlers and Trust

something to do with not being transparent. Most of the great corporate and political scandals of the modern age have had more to do with cover-ups than with the original act of wrongdoing itself.

In contrast, people and organizations that are transparent in their actions are the ones that consistently grow and come out ahead in the long run. Those who are forthcoming with information—good and bad—can more effectively lead a team to accomplish great things.

An organization itself can and should be transparent, but to be so it needs leaders who are transparent in their actions. An active beehive hanging in a tree looks to me as ominous as the Death Star in a *Star Wars* movie. I definitely don't trust it. But have you ever seen a cross section of a beehive? By placing it behind glass we can see the fascinating inner workings of an efficient organization. Somehow, knowing what each of those busy bees is up to puts my mind at ease.

Employees, customers, vendors, and shareholders know what to expect from transparent leaders. Fostering transparency takes commitment and confidence. It can be tempting to hide problems, but the transparent leader knows that the truth eventually slips out anyway—and often looks worse than it did originally. As an ancient Eastern adage says, "Three things cannot be hidden forever: the sun, the moon, and the truth."

Mix It Up!

Project authenticity to gain TRUST. Tap into the power of individuals and understand that they are more wary of leaders than ever before. The only logical response is for you to get real to earn their TRUST.

Chapter 6

Some Shocking Behavior

Philip Zimbardo and his buddy Stanley Milgram were undoubtedly laughing one spring day in 1950. The high school seniors at James Monroe High School in the Bronx, New York, were nearing graduation. Zimbardo had spent the previous year as a shunned outsider at North Hollywood High School. (He later learned that there had been a rumor he was from a mafia family.) This year, however, he had been chosen "Jimmy Monroe"—the student body's pick as the most popular kid in the class.

Zimbardo and Milgram found it laughable that a kid could transform from one extreme to another in such a short time. They both reached the conclusion that Zimbardo had not changed. The situation had changed.

Situational psychology would play a major role in both boys' lives. Milgram, the son of Jewish immigrants escaping persecution in Europe, conducted one of the twentieth century's most famous psychological experiments. In an effort to better understand the "we were just following orders" defense of Nazi war criminals, Milgram set out to measure the willingness of average people to perform acts that conflicted with their own personal consciences. His friend Zimbardo, also a second-generation immigrant, later conducted an equally famous experiment studying the effects of obedience and authority. The Milgram experiment and Zimbardo's Stanford prison experiment can arguably be described as the most influential, controversial, and well-known research into the nature of behavior in an organizational setting.

Milgram's experiment was rather simple. Subjects were led to believe that they were participating in a study on how people learn. Little did they know that they were the ones actually being studied—everyone else involved in the experiment was part of a ruse. Each participant was asked to administer an ever-increasing electrical shock to another "volunteer learner" as punishment for answering questions incorrectly. No actual shocks were administered, but test subjects believed that they were. (The "learners" were actors who feigned increasing levels of pain with every jolt.)

Participants were told that the shocks they administered started at a relatively low 15 volts. Many test subjects would hesitate to continue upon reaching 135 volts. However, once assured that they would not be held responsible for their actions and that the officials would take care of the learners' medical needs, all continued with their zapping behavior. Incredibly, 65 percent of experiment subjects delivered the ultimate 450-volt shock, despite seeing and hearing the excruciating pain they were inflicting. Not one refused to administer shocks before reaching the 300-volt level, even though they were provided with a chart that showed this level being just short of causing "extreme intensity shock."

These were randomly selected, regular guys. Despite expressing empathy for their victims, they would continue to inflict harm simply because a perceived authority figure in a lab coat was asking them politely to "Please continue." They were free to leave the experiment at any time, but they didn't.

Future variations on the experiments proved that variables such as gender, locale, and even the inference that the learner had "a heart problem" didn't significantly alter the outcome of the original findings. Dr. Thomas Blass, a professor in the University of Maryland system, has studied every subsequent attempt to replicate Milgram's shocking experiment. He found that throughout the world 61 to 66 percent of people are full-voltage shockers, very close to the statistical range of the original experiment. When test subjects were allowed to give verbal commands to someone else, as opposed to actually physically throwing the switch themselves—in other words, when they took on the role of a manager—willingness to administer the full 450 volts of juice increased to over 90 percent!

41

Some Shocking Behavior

Yikes! Talk about pointless and stupid behavior. Yet a growth leader cannot ignore this strong tendency for people to blindly conform to even the most destructive practices. Despite people's professed ethical convictions, authority figures will always find it very easy to pull the strings of their subjugated puppets.

Ten years after the original study, Milgram's old friend Zimbardo conducted an equally simple and profound experiment at Stanford University. Seventy-five young men responded to a newspaper ad offering money to take part in a two-week "prison simulation." This list was whittled down to 24 by Zimbardo's team, based on who was deemed to be the most "mentally healthy."

The experiment began to unravel after only two days and was forced to shut down after six. Both guards and prisoners quickly assumed the worst aspects of their arbitrarily assigned roles. Guards became increasingly sadistic, while prisoners quickly showed signs of despair and hopelessness.

When placed in even a mock prison environment, these seemingly well-adjusted participants quickly exhibited extreme behavior. We're talking about some pretty crazy stuff here: prisoner revolts, hunger strikes, use of pain as punishment, revoked paroles, solitary confinement, and physical humiliation. Don't forget, these were supposedly the most mentally healthy ones!

Even Zimbardo, who had appointed himself prison warden, fell victim to the role identity crisis. On day four, upon hearing of a rumored prison break, he tried (albeit unsuccessfully) to move the experiment from a Stanford basement to a local jail. Luckily, these actual prison officials weren't part of the deteriorating experiment.

It took an outside observer to bring the fiasco to an end. Zimbardo's graduate student girlfriend and future wife stopped by to conduct subject interviews. Repulsed by the overall conditions, she immediately recognized the inhumane nature of the experiment. She eventually convinced Zimbardo to shut it down.

At some level the test subjects always knew that this was just a simulation, yet they apparently couldn't stop themselves from behaving in wholly inappropriate manners. Remember, this was all staged and supposedly controlled. Imagine what's possible in the uncontrolled world we live in.

It's easy to dismiss these experiments as mere academic anecdotes. You may be saying to yourself, "Okay, they're interesting, but what do they have to do with delivering Milkshake Moments? What possible relevance do these experiments have for me today?"

In the spring of 2007, advanced placement high school freshmen in Waxahachie, Texas, took part in

Some Shocking Behavior

a three-week learning simulation designed to better understand intolerance during the Holocaust. Students were randomly assigned roles as "Germans" and "Jews." Allegedly, the "German" students hit, spat upon, and publicly degraded the "Jewish" students. A learning experience meant to teach the "ills of discrimination" degenerated back into patterns eerily reminiscent of the dark period they were studying.

Here's another recent variation that's even more disturbing. David Stuart, a 37-year-old Floridian, was arrested for a series of prank calls. Over a 10-year period starting in 1994, Mr. Stuart (no relation to our would-be milkshake maker) placed dozens of calls to fast-food restaurants, prodding managers to interrogate young female employees. By pretending to be a police officer, he was able to persuade store managers and other employees to conduct ludicrously inappropriate acts involving these vulnerable young women. His calls led to strip searches, physical beatings, and sexual abuse of the so-called suspects, with 70 documented cases occurring from Juneau, Alaska, to Hinsdale, Georgia.

Here's the crazy thing: Mr. Stuart was never physically in any of these locations. He was simply a supposed authority figure on the other end of a phone line. Experts commenting on this perpetrator's actions noted that he likely targeted fast-food outlets because they tend to have rigid, highly structured cultures that embrace uniformity.

These managers knew exactly how long french fries were to stay in the fryer and how many times restrooms were to be inspected in a given day. But there was nothing in their employee manual that would prepare them for an authoritative voice demanding employee strip searches.

Then of course there are the recent events at the Abu Ghraib prison in Iraq. While we may never know who was ultimately responsible for the guards' egregious errors in judgment, the shocking pictures alone tell an all-too-familiar tale.

The Milgram and Zimbardo experiments, as well as these more recent examples, point to an important commonality in human behavior. The drive for organizational conformity can cause almost anyone to lose their moral compass and ability to think rationally. Yet rational thinking is one of the key ingredients of any Milkshake Moment. Before his death in 1984, Stanley Milgram himself said, "When an individual merges . . . into an organizational structure, a new creature replaces autonomous man, unhindered by the limitations of individual morality, freed of human inhibition, mindful only of the sanctions of authority."

Obviously the sadistic behavior of the shockers and the guards is disturbing. But equally troubling is the sheeplike mentality of the victims. Whatever one's role, we all must understand that the power of conformity can

45

create limitless havoc within any organizational setting. Mindless conformity certainly doesn't lead to growth.

As a growth leader, it is incumbent upon you to keep a constant vigil with regard to these phenomena. Are there sadist-like managers in your organization? Do you know how many within the ranks of your work-force feel hopelessly powerless? Are you able to take a stand against both the "guards" and the "prisoners" you encounter and say, "Hey, your behavior isn't helping us get where we want to go"? What happens to someone in your organization who questions the detached voice of authority? Will you refuse to throw the switch when your conscience sounds an alarm?

The absurdity of human conformity can truly be a puzzle. Human behavior often leads to head-shaking incredulity.

In researching these two experiments, I was often reminded of how it feels when I get invited into the inner sanctum of many organizations. It frequently seems as if I've stumbled into the middle of a lunatic cult. I haven't been there long enough to drink their conformity Kool-Aid, and therefore their words and deeds strike me as, well, laughable—sad, frightening, and counterproductive, but nevertheless laughable.

Speaking of laughable, do you think Milgram and Zimbardo would laugh to learn that the fast-food targeting

David Stuart was a former Florida corrections officer? While there is nothing funny about his depravity, my guess is that knowing Mr. Stuart had been a former prison guard would not shock either one of them.

Mix It Up!

Keep your eyes open for blind conformity. Neither shockers or shockees can deliver Milkshake Moments. It's the individuals who have the courage to speak out against the status quo who foster growth.

Chapter 7

Lessons from the Cubicle Farm

Movies have the power to fundamentally impact our views on almost any aspect of life. For instance, *Animal House* forever changed how people perceive fraternities. To this day, golfers still quote lines from *Caddyshack*. No matter how much my parents wax nostalgic about their teen years, *Grease* and *American Graffiti* are how I've come to view the 1950s. A few years ago the owner of a Turkish travel agency told me that the movie *Midnight Express*—the story of a young American drug smuggler locked up in a horrific Turkish prison—still shows up as a prevalent reason why Americans say they would be less than likely to ever visit Turkey.

Despite all having been released more than 25 years ago, these movies have had a tremendous impact on our collective psyches. Movies create perceptions, and perceptions become realities.

At the close of the millennium, another movie came out that is already having an equally profound impact upon your reality (whether you know it now or not). The movie *Office Space* has come to define the modern workplace.

Young software engineer Peter Gibbons works for Initech, a generic high-tech company that could be based in any suburban office park in the United States. Peter hates his job almost as much as his co-workers do. From the Indian-American Samir Nagheenanajar, who complains that nobody ever pronounces his name properly, to the middle-aged mumbler Milton, who was laid off years ago but was never informed, these hapless souls struggle to survive in a hierarchical hell.

Peter's greatest source of frustration is the boss Lumbergh, a passive-aggressive, white-collar middle manager who mindlessly speaks at Peter, not with him. The plot thickens with the introduction of two outside consultants known as "The Bobs," brought in to rightsize Initech. For Peter and his associates, this means that their jobs are clearly in jeopardy.

Office Space featured Jennifer Aniston, star of TV megahit *Friends*, and was directed by Mike Judge, who had previously scored big with animated TV comedies *Beavis and Butt-Head* and *King of the Hill*. Despite all this momentum, the movie barely made a blip at the box office, narrowly recouping its modest $10 million budget.

But this was the little comedy that could. Thanks to snowballing word of mouth and relentless TV airings, it took on a life of its own. It eventually sold over six million copies on video and is still going strong. *Office Space*'s impact on today's work culture is enormous. The term *TPS report* has become synonymous with mindless paperwork in offices everywhere. "Going *Office Space*" on something is now a popular term referring to the lead characters' ceremonious destruction of a constantly malfunctioning copy machine. The real-world company Swingline had not sold a red stapler (a prominent plot device in the movie) for years, but the company reintroduced the color as the movie's popularity grew and red stapler demand spiked.

In hindsight, it's easy now to see why *Office Space* became what *Entertainment Weekly* has called a "stealth blockbuster." It has hit a nerve with today's young workforce. The movie was purposely shot in a style that conveyed a soul-sucking, dehumanizing environment. The overall feel of the film is a combination of two other 25+-year-old classics—*2001: A Space Odyssey* and *One Flew over the Cuckoo's Nest*. While at one level *Office Space* works as a standard farce, themes of alienation and helplessness can be found in all three films. Even the antiseptic space is part of the story: The lighting is artificial, and so is the overall environment. As each movie unfolds, the characters behave increasingly more like rats trapped in a cage.

51

Lessons from the Cubicle Farm

The villain in these films isn't a ranting, raving tyrant. Instead, it is the infuriatingly calm and seemingly rational voice of reason that pushes our protagonists to the edge. The inauthentic, superficial Lumbergh uses the same lilting, condescending tone as *Space Odyssey*'s HAL the computer and *Cuckoo's Nest*'s Nurse Ratchett. For all three, their forced politeness and banal banter are far more frustrating than the more commonly portrayed screaming, red-faced boss. Lumbergh arrogantly ignores what his employees are telling him and just keeps repeating his mantras: "Yeahhhh . . . did you see the memo on this?" and "Yeahhhh, I'm also going to need you to go ahead and come in on Saturday."

From the moment Peter enters Initech's cubicle farm, it is eerily similar to an insane asylum or a soulless spaceship guided by a talking computer. Peter is no longer a person. He is an automaton that cranks out meaningless TPS reports. All of the work and the processes portrayed involve mind-numbing details. Whenever he tries to explain himself to superiors, he is met with a canned response straight from Mismanagement 301.

People laugh at *Office Space* because it's only slightly more ludicrous than what they see around them. And it's not just offices. People who work in warehouses, construction sites, and retail shops can all relate to the familiar themes. If you are a leader who hasn't watched this movie, I suggest you do it soon. It is a funny movie, but you'll also come to better understand how many people, especially younger workers, feel about supervisors and work in general.

For an entire generation, this movie and the newer, similarly themed TV series *The Office* are their reality. (At the time of writing this book, the latest season of *The Office* was the best-selling DVD on Amazon.) This is what my teenage son expects to encounter when he goes to work in an organization: a place where your individuality gets subverted, your drive gets deflated, your co-workers are backstabbing loons, and you report to a boss who cares only about pointless policies and procedures. This kind of work environment is perceived as the coal mine of the modern age; instead of black lung disease you get black soul disease.

The tagline for this movie was a very simple one: "Work Sucks." That's today's stark perception, and therefore reality, in many organizations. Don't let yours be one of them. Managers are telling today's workers to "think outside the box" and yet keep sticking them in cubicles.

I'm not calling for the literal plowing under of the cubicle farm. Instead, I am suggesting that growth leaders always find innovative ways to help individuals see that what they do really matters.

Mix It Up!

Focus on creating an environment where human beings can thrive. Systems can, at best, only deliver efficiency. You need engaged human beings to deliver Milkshake Moments.

Chapter 8

The Managed

People in supervisory roles should be leaders. "Should be" is the operative phrase here, because in most situations, managers aren't really leaders—rather, they're functionaries, operatives, utilitarian taskmasters. Whenever I interact with another human being in any type of transaction, it is obvious to me who is being managed and who is being led. Consider the tale of two eateries.

I recently went to a nice Italian restaurant in a major metropolitan area in Middle America. My party of five walked in the front door, approached the hostess stand, and immediately noticed two things. The restaurant was full and the hostess was missing. This was my gathering, and I felt responsible for securing a table as quickly as possible. The full dining room was to my right. The bar's completely empty seating area was immediately to my left. I made an executive decision to direct my group to the unoccupied tables.

55

However, we encountered a slight snag. All the tables were set for four, and we were five. Naturally, I saw a simple solution anyone would have no doubt seen as well: "Let's just push these two adjoining tables together." That's when all the trouble started.

"Sir! Sir! Sir! You can't do that, Sir!" Wow. One logical maneuver and I was hit with a barrage of "Sir bombs" from the assistant bar manager. "Sir" can be a polite word, of course, but we all recognized that in this context her use of the word "Sir" was actually internal code for "Jerkface." ("Ma'am" bombs deliver a similar payload.)

When I came into the restaurant I think I was Mr. Little, but she let me know very quickly that I was in fact now a sir. Clearly I was being reprimanded in front of my entire party. I didn't have a chance to explain or apologize. "Sir" bombs were exploding all around me. She proceeded to expound on "You can't do that, Sir!" in more detail. The obvious question is, of course, why not?

Why can't I do that? I'll admit I don't know for sure, but I have a pretty good guess. It was a management rule, and rules can't be broken.

This rule probably came about in a staff meeting. The irritable general manager was in a finger-pointing mood. Who, he needed to know, was responsible for the table being overturned by the drunken, boisterous party of 16 rugby hooligans the weekend before? He probably admonished the entire staff with a blanket warning of "Don't let these customers push you around. If they try to move the tables, just tell them they can't do it."

Suddenly, any employee who allows a customer to reconfigure predetermined seating designs is a wimp and "not a team player." It's an "us versus them" mentality, and you can't let "them" (i.e., customers) push you around.

Eventually we got the tables all worked out and the food got rave reviews from my party. Yet the damage had been done. For me, the "sir" bomb shrapnel stung throughout the meal. It didn't matter how good the food was; I already had a bad taste in my mouth. I have returned to this city many times, but I will always steer clear of this particular restaurant.

Clearly this assistant manager was just that, a manager. She had been taught that adhering to internal rules is more important than finding a way to make customers feel welcome. It's as if the restaurant's mission statement reads:

It is our goal here at Don's Little Italy to create and maintain a perfectly balanced system of symmetrical table placement within a geometrical grid. We strive to be the industry leader in symmetrical table placement. We will empower our employees to manage any situation that threatens proper table configuration.

57

The Managed

Mix It Up!

Remember that a manager's mission should never solely focus on the internal. More often than not, Milkshake Moments can only be judged by the external world.

Chapter 9

The Led

Let's contrast this frontline interaction from the past chapter with another recent experience I had in a different major metropolitan area in Middle America. This story begins with me arriving early for a particularly important dinner meeting. I walked in and immediately saw a dining room to my left and a bar with a seating area to my right. I explained to the hostess that I was early, and she suggested I wait at the bar until my party arrived.

The hostess escorted me into the bar area and told the other gathered employees, "This gentleman is early for his reservation, and it's his first time here. Please make him feel welcome." That's when Beatrice went into full-on service mode.

"Hi, my name is Beatrice. Welcome to Sam's Steak House! What's your name?"

"Steve Little," I quickly replied.

"Would you prefer 'Steve' or 'Mr. Little'?" she then asked.

"Steve is fine," I answered.

"Okay, Steve, it's a pleasure to meet you. You're going to love it here. Can I start you off with a cold beverage?"

One beer and one orange juice later, I had come to observe how Beatrice, despite having a title of bar manager, was also a gifted growth leader. The bar was pretty full, and people were regularly leaving the area either to grab a table or to head home. As they left, every patron departed with a personalized good-bye from Beatrice. "Thanks for coming, Harold. See you next time! Enjoy your dinner, Maria and Heather! Happy anniversary, Mr. and Mrs. Ramsey!"

"What a great place," I thought. It obviously attracted a steady stream of regulars. Friends were regaling one another with tall tales. The big game was on the big-screen TV. Everyone was smiling and laughing. Thanks to ringmaster Beatrice, we all sensed that we were part of her big show. It was just a regular weeknight, but, thanks to Beatrice, it felt like a party.

As my prearranged meeting time grew closer, I asked Beatrice for the tab. While she was punching the register, I asked her how she could remember so many of her regulars' names. She replied, "What makes you think they're regulars?"

"I just assumed you already knew all these people," I said. "You all seem so familiar with each other."

"Actually, I've never met any of these people before tonight," she said.

I was both flabbergasted and intrigued. Questions started pouring out of me. "You mean to tell me that you know everyone's name in this bar? How do you do it? I can't even remember my own name sometimes. Why do you do it? What's his name? And her name? What's in a Harvey Wallbanger? What did the Ramseys have to drink? What is the home team's record so far this season?"

Amazingly, Beatrice had the right answer for all my inquiries. Eventually I was seated with my party, but I couldn't stop thinking about this incredible bar manager. Twice during dinner I got up and posed more questions. When I left, I gave her my card and asked her to e-mail me. Hers was a story that needed telling.

It came as no surprise to me to learn that Beatrice was no ordinary barkeep. A few years prior to my encounter with her, Beatrice had caught the eye of corporate management in the chain. She became an "opener," traveling the country training new bar staff whenever the growing chain opened a new location.

Beatrice enjoyed both the work and the travel for a time, but eventually came to realize she really missed the camaraderie of working with one group of staffers every day and actually serving the public. Beatrice asked those above if she could return to a bar manager's position, and it appears everybody has won. It was better for me, it was better for the growing chain, and it was better for Beatrice.

Beatrice's leaders recognized that she would be a greater asset to the organization doing what she wanted to do. A lesser group of managers might have forced her to stay in the corporate training position. But Beatrice is being led, not managed.

Our assistant bar manager at the Italian restaurant and Beatrice the barkeep at the steak house have essentially the same job. The difference is, Beatrice isn't afraid of those above her and she doesn't view me as the potential enemy. The two have the same job, but completely different attitudes and therefore results.

Beatrice gladly made me a milkshake for dessert that night. (It was on the menu and I couldn't resist.) I'm also willing to bet that if she had caught me rearranging her tables, she would have thanked me for helping her as opposed to reprimanding me for customer insubordination.

Mix It Up!

Find growth-oriented individuals who want to be led and lead them. Managers hire and try to control; leaders inspire around a goal.

(Extra Toppings)

Accept that tension is inherent in any organization

Homeostasis is defined as "a state of psychological equilibrium obtained when tension or drive has been reduced or eliminated." Too many trendy management techniques seek to eliminate the creative tension that is necessary for growth.

Recognize that the information age rewards thinking

Perhaps there was a time when all that mattered was efficiency. In today's world, ideas garner the most value. True leaders know that idea generation is rarely efficient, and growth initiatives are fueled by the random flow of human innovation.

Don't waste your time managing the cash cow

It should be relatively easy to hire milkers for what works today. It's a growth leader's job to raise the calves with the most potential for tomorrow.

Section 3
Put Purpose Before Profit

Milkshake Moments are most likely to occur when growth leaders concentrate their time, money, and effort on cultivating a strong sense of purpose.

Some recent studies and surveys have shown that approximately two-thirds of American employees don't see a connection between what they do and how it fits into the overall purpose of the organization. In my observations, this percentage sounds rather low. That is to say, at least 80 percent of the employees I encounter appear to have no idea how their job fits into a grander sense of the organization's purpose.

To gauge the role purpose plays into your organization, ask yourself these questions:

- Whom is your organization trying to serve?
- Do the people in the organization understand whom you are trying to serve?
- What is your organization trying to accomplish over the long term?
- What unique strengths does your organization possess and value?
- What gets you out of bed in the morning?
- What gets your people out of bed in the morning?

While all of these questions are important, it's the last one that holds the most interest for me. People care about what gets them out of bed in the morning. Animals don't care and machines don't care. Computers don't care. People do. Instilling people with a sense of purpose starts with growth leaders. Growth leaders set the sense of purpose for their organization and then allow it to permeate throughout. To be perceived as a champion of growth, your job is to continually reiterate this common purpose to those who work with and for you.

And remember, while a sense of purpose can manifest itself in an organization in an infinite number of ways, there is one consistent maxim on which you can rely: Organizational purpose should never be about money.

Chapter 10

It's Never about Money

Don't misunderstand. Money is a great way to keep score. Money is the fuel for expansion. Money is an effective way to benchmark and reward success. It doesn't matter if you're a business, a nonprofit, a school board, or a Girl Scout troop. It takes money to further your cause. Many organizations, from businesses to nonprofits, often lose sight of this irrefutable truth. The executive director of a chamber of commerce once told me, "'Nonprofit' is our tax status . . . it's never our goal."

However, over the long haul, money alone won't get you or anyone else out of bed. If you've lost the passion for what you do, it doesn't matter how much you're getting paid.

(You don't have to have a lot of passion for everything you do, but you'd better have a passion for everything you do a lot of.)

If it's not about money, what is it about? For any organization interested in reaching another level, establishing a unique purpose should be the starting point. A growth leader should be able to articulate a clear and concise statement of the organization's true aspirations. It must be understood by all those who share an interest, from employees to customers and from vendors to shareholders. Purpose always precedes profits.

Let me ask you a question. Other than someone you know personally, who is the first person who comes to mind when you read the word *hero*? Take a second, close your eyes, and think of an individual the word conjures up in your mind.

Now, let me ask you a couple of questions about your hero.

First, is your hero someone known primarily for wealth accumulation? This is a question I've asked literally thousands of organizational leaders over the past few years. Rarely do people name a rich person as their hero. Sure, every once in a while someone will name Bill Gates, Warren Buffett, or Ted Turner as their hero. However, when I dig a little deeper, the reason they are held up as heroes is often for their reputation as philanthropists. Indeed, they're known for giving money away more than for accumulating it. Heroes fascinate me.

Mix It Up!

Measure beyond money. Ultimately, profit and loss statements aren't enough to get even accountants out of bed.

Chapter 11

The Wizard of Westwood

While far from being a uniquely American trait, Americans sure do love their heroes. We needed heroes at our country's founding and we've kept seeking them out ever since. From George Washington to Eleanor Roosevelt to Martin Luther King Jr., the mythology surrounding our heroes is deeply embedded in our national psyche. At its core, our idea of a hero is the person who has honesty, integrity, and authenticity. Our heroes transcend their own self-interest and manage to serve a greater good.

While I've always been fascinated by the evolution of the hero in our culture, one of my greatest frustrations is the inability to actually meet heroic figures. I can read their words and in some cases even hear their voices, but so many of my heroes have left this earth. And while I have a few heroes who are still alive, the world has just become so crowded that it is nearly impossible to meet any public figure, much less a true hero.

A few years ago, however, I got to meet a hero of mine. They call him the Wizard of Westwood.

The Wizard was born in southern Indiana in 1910. A good student and an even better athlete, he helped lead his high school basketball team to a state championship in 1927. He continued his basketball career at Purdue University, where he was named three times to the All-American team. In his senior year, he led the Boilermakers to a national championship.

After graduating from Purdue, armed with a bachelor's degree in English, the newly married young man entered Indiana State Teachers College, where he earned a master's degree in education. He then became both a teacher and a coach at the high school level in Kentucky and Indiana until, like most young men of his time, he served in the military after the attack on Pearl Harbor.

A few years after the war, the Wizard was invited by Indiana State Teachers College (now called Indiana State University) to serve as athletic director and head basketball coach. His basketball team's two-year 47 and 14 won-lost record earned him national recognition. Soon the big schools were courting the coach, and he eventually got hitched with the University of California–Los Angeles at its Westwood campus. That was when the magic started for the Wizard.

At UCLA, this man named John Wooden became a basketball legend:

- Ten national championships.

- Twenty-three Pacific-10 championships.

- Four perfect 30–0 seasons.

- An unprecedented 88-game winning streak.

There's no question that he was the greatest college basketball coach in history. For many, including myself, he was the greatest coach in American sports history, period (with all due respect to my friends in both Green Bay and Alabama, who recently booed this pronouncement in a good-natured way). It doesn't matter if you know basketball—or even sports in general, for that matter. The point here is that as a young man, I grew up with a love of the game of basketball, and Coach Wooden embodied all that was good about the game. In a word, he was my hero.

In March of 2005, I got to meet the Wizard.

Coach Wooden was the keynote speaker at a conference I was attending. As someone who speaks at over 100 general sessions a year, I normally stay close to the exits when I'm not onstage. But on this day I planned to

The Wizard of Westwood

be front and center. Wooden was to speak at lunch, and that morning I asked the conference director if it would be possible for me to meet the coach. I spent a full hour with Coach Wooden before and again after he spoke to an audience of over 1,000 people. The experience far exceeded my expectations.

Coach was 95 years young. While he had lost a few steps physically (he walked with a cane and sat in a chair onstage), he had not lost one step mentally. He was as sharp at 95 as most of us are at 35. It was incredible to watch this slight, soft-spoken man hold the audience in the palm of his hand. For over an hour he engrossed me and everyone else assembled with tales relating to one's underlying sense of purpose. He was the furthest thing from a motivational speaker, yet no one could have left there without feeling genuinely inspired.

I honestly don't remember exactly what Coach said to me one-on-one versus those things he said while onstage. What I do know is that my hero left me with two lessons I'll never forget. The first was this: He said, "I never set out to win championships. I always knew that I wanted to help young people achieve beyond their own expecta-tions of themselves. Championships were a by-product of that effort."

I later learned that of the hundreds of players the Wizard had coached throughout his career, he has lost track of only a handful. Ask him about some of his favorites and they're always the unheralded players who went on to accomplish great things in their lives. Coach was a coach in the greatest sense of the word. He cared about his kids first, and his kids have never stopped caring about him. It's an amazing experience when your heroes live up to your expectations of them.

The second lesson I learned that day I'm going to save for later. Just know that my hero never disappoints, and his lessons are worth waiting for.

Mix It Up!

Focus on a worthy purpose. It is the only way you will consistently win in the game of growth.

Chapter 12

Profit Pushers

For most of my life I've been involved in music. I sang in bands, I managed bands, I financed bands, and I have seen more bands than I care to remember. While never my real job, it has always been about as strong an avocation as one can imagine. Somehow, like an addictive drug, it was something I just couldn't give up.

Call it a midlife crisis or a case of Peter Pan syndrome, but somehow I found myself once again fronting rock bands from the mid-1990s until just a few years ago.

It will probably come as no shock to you that illicit drugs are a part of the rock and roll world. In my youth, I made a deal with myself that the music would be more important to me than the party. I chose to abstain, but the substances were always around me.

I couldn't help but notice the changes in these substances over the years. In my youth, "drugs" were mysterious concoctions packaged in little clear plastic bags

79

and in aluminum foil that had been folded one too many times. By the 1990s these types of street drugs were no longer in vogue. Everywhere I looked, I saw prescription bottles and branded tablets. The new high had become legitimately manufactured substances used in an illegitimate way.

One day in the late 1990s I first heard the word OxyContin while sitting in a club waiting to take the stage. "OxyContin? Is that a new brand of Band-Aids?" I wondered aloud. I soon came to learn that this synthetic opiate was a ticking time bomb ready to explode.

Within months of having heard of the drug and learning of the tragedies left in its wake, I met the owner of two methadone clinics in the Southeast. He explained to me that his business was no longer there to help intravenous drug users: 80 percent of his clients were now addicted to synthetic opiates, with OxyContin at the top of the list. We now know that this phenomenon was playing out in communities throughout the United States. What started out as a rural Appalachian scourge quickly moved to suburbs across the country.

What happens when an individual or organization is in it only for the money and loses sight of the greater purpose? Perhaps one day Michael Friedman, Howard R. Udell, and Dr. Paul D. Goldenheim can tell us all.

The Milkshake Moment

These three men are the former executives of Purdue Pharma, maker of this highly addictive drug OxyContin, an overprescribed painkiller that has decimated countless families and communities in the United States. In 2007, these three executives pleaded guilty to misleading the public and were fined $634 million for intentionally understating the drug's addictive properties. (The company paid $600 million, while the executives themselves are on the hook for the rest.) They were also sentenced to 400 hours each of community service.

A Roanoke, Virginia, newspaper headline read, "Hillbilly Heroin's Pushers Escape Prison." Perhaps one day I'll come to understand the stupid system that allows these guys to walk, while thousands of Americans are locked up for years in our nation's prisons on simple possession charges, with no intent to be pushers. But that's an issue for another day. Let's get back to Purdue Pharma.

There was big money to be made pushing these little pills, and it was Purdue Pharma's one-trick pony. According to the *New York Times*, at one point the drug made up 90 percent of the company's sales, with over 6.5 million prescriptions written a year. By 2001, revenues stood at $1.5 billion despite mounting awareness of the problem around the country. Executives reportedly faked scientific findings, had their sales force lie to doctors, and repeatedly claimed in the media that the wonderful thing about this drug was that patients wouldn't get hooked on it.

Any Appalachian police officer could have told you years before that their false claims were a joke. Back surgery patients, after three months of taking doctor-prescribed OxyContin, were pawning their valuables to feed their habits. Teenagers were holding up pharmacies and stealing only the OxyContin, leaving the cash and other merchandise behind. Emergency room visits related to prescriptive painkillers tripled within six years of the drug's introduction. A national survey found that 975,000 people reported using OxyContin for nonmedical use. Community officials, doctors, the media, and even the company's own salespeople were sounding warning alarms about what was happening.

I'm no doctor, but it is an opiate, right? How could they keep denying it was addictive? How could these guys get out of bed and look themselves in the mirror every day?

What was Purdue Pharma's purpose? Was it to "promote health and healing," or was it to rake in as much cash as possible, as quickly as possible? Unlike Enron or WorldCom, these executives couldn't pin the blame on some impenetrable accounting practices or some rogue middle managers. It was criminal obfuscation of the highest order. These executives knew their cash cow was highly addictive and continued to tell everyone exactly the opposite. They did whatever would keep the money rolling in.

Purdue Pharma was founded in the 1890s by well-intentioned professionals looking to profitably produce safe and effective pain relievers, a noble purpose by any measure. How did the organization manage to stray so far from its original reason for being?

Some say money is the root of all evil. I don't know if that's true, but I'm sure that's how this organization lost its way. There was nothing inherently evil about this medical compound. When used properly, it is a safe and effective pain reliever. But these pushers weren't happy with a sustainable $100 million or $200 million niche drug for those suffering from intense short-term pain. They lied for years in order to make more money, more quickly. They didn't simply lose sight of their purpose; they consciously perverted it, and millions suffered as a result.

Mix It Up!

Always do the right thing. It's not just an ethical imperative; it's the clearest path for sustained growth.

Chapter 13

NoClu Motors, Inc.

There are times when bad people consciously do bad things in organizations. More often, good people with the best of intentions lose sight of their purpose and don't even realize that they are so caught up in fighting today's battle that they forget the overall objectives. The executives at Purdue Pharma were outright criminals. The only thing criminal about this next story is the squandering of a real opportunity.

For decades the United States has been the most powerful economic force in the world. In the early 1950s, with the rest of the world decimated by World War II, the United States represented over half the world's output of goods and services. From structural steel to children's cartoons, the United States was the undisputed king of commerce. Arguably our greatest source of national pride was the American automobile industry. By the 1970s it had consolidated into what became known as the Big Three, a triumvirate that ruled the domestic market until a steady decline turned into a meltdown over the past decade.

Somewhere along the line the rest of the world apparently retooled. The Germans, the Japanese, the Swedes, and later even the Koreans got in on the game. Despite our continued economic superiority, the Big Three have come to symbolize our nation's lack of economic invincibility. Some really smart people have tried a lot of seemingly smart things, yet the only big thing about the Big Three over the past 25 years has been the size of their decline in market share. In 1999 the Big Three had a 71 percent market share in the United States. By 2005 that share had dropped to 58 percent, and by August 2007 less than half of the automobiles sold in the United States were from one of the Big Three.

America's declining automotive industry is a pretty touchy subject. There are undoubtedly a lot of reasons for it, and I'll be the first to admit I am far from an expert on it—remember I'm a *growth* expert. Yet based on my recent experience with one of these Big Three companies, I have come to better understand their predicament.

Not too long ago, one of the Big Three (we'll call it NoClu Motors), invited me to help grow one of their divisions. Eventually I was asked to visit the NoClu headquarters.

Everything looked great. All the cubicles appeared to have a logical layout and there was a quiet, steady hum to the place. I'm still not sure if that hum was coming from the workforce or the fluorescent tubes overhead. I do distinctly remember that the corporate cafeteria was particularly well appointed.

My first day with NoClu was spent in a state-of-the-art boardroom with a handful of director-level executives who averaged 20+ years in the NoClu fold. I was quite proud of the observations and recommendations I had developed for the team. My recommendations were specific, action-able, and well supported by both internal and external data I had acquired.

On day one, it was clear that my ideas were being well received. At the end of the day, I asked the team for a few pieces of missing data, and we all agreed to recon-vene in the same boardroom the following morning to put our great new plan in motion.

Day two was the beginning of the end of our relation-ship. My recommendations regarding sales force compen-sation plans, marketing initiatives, and vertical integration of industry-specific product features were shot down before my first cup of coffee.

At NoClu, middle managers apparently still play the ridiculous game of "beat the bosses to work." I rolled in at the previously appointed time of 9:00 A.M. believing that we were ready to roll up our sleeves and get some real work done. Little did I know that a couple of hours prior to my arrival, informal presentations had already been given internally and "the big boys upstairs" had already put the kibosh on our elegant new strategy.

Somehow my fearless group of gung-ho go-getters had come down with a debilitating strain of the common corporate virus known as *theywontletus*, a Latin word that can be loosely translated as "I have a second mortgage and a college-bound kid who needs braces."

These same people, who just the previous day had been invigorated by the opportunities afforded through change, were now sneezing and coughing back at me. I heard nothing but anemic excuses as to why none of these ideas could work in practice. Nobody had the strength to stand up and say, "We have identified a viable market. Let's build a system to meet it." Instead they were stymied by a perceived inability to shoehorn our plans for growth into their existing structure. Besides, the higher-ups always know best.

It was so disheartening. It is not overstating it to say that it felt as if I was talking to the leaders of a communist-run cooperative. Ultimately, their only concern was keeping the production monster fed. Everything was about units of throughput, organizational hierarchy, and playing it safe.

According to NoClu's annual report that year, its driving purpose included complete customer satisfaction, operational excellence, innovative design, and superior quality, all achieved through the power of teamwork. Ultimately, these were just words on a page. This team had no intention whatsoever of meeting their organization's stated purpose. By the end of day two, I had preemptively fired myself.

How sad. A group of veteran cubicle dwellers had actually seen the light of new opportunity. They had all the right ingredients, but they weren't willing to risk a Milkshake Moment.

Mix It Up!

Identify your most optimal opportunities and then structure your organization around them. Recognize that when an organization begins to look for reasons why they can't do something, they actually start the slide toward not doing anything.

Chapter 14

Purpose in the Plan

In 2002, the Vancouver, Canada, Board of Trade was having a tough time. Membership in the chamber of commerce-like organization had been falling ever so slightly for years and now sat at just 4,000 members. Like a lot of community-based organizations, it was fighting a trend of general disengagement.

Many felt that for the Board of Trade to simply stop its bleeding would have been quite an accomplishment, but new Managing Director Darcy Rezac felt this wasn't good enough. He aimed to grow. His team decided that the antidote to disengagement was engagement. They decided to stress the association's role in the essential skill of developing relationships. This was a rather novel approach since most trade associations tend to trumpet their value in fostering referrals—the traditional transactional networking approach.

Rezac's team used a collaborative approach that involved the board, staffers, members, and even outside facilitators. They focused on three key words: engagement, value, and service. Their purpose was to grow membership by proving the value of the organization to the Vancouver community overall. They identified three goals that would serve this purpose. Their goals were quantifiable, bold, and realistic.

1. Increase membership from 4,000 to 5,000 members within three years, with long-term retention of 92 percent.
2. Impact policy changes such as specific business-property tax reductions, streamlined border-access procedures, a balanced provincial budget, and a push for federal spending on domestic growth initiatives.
3. Launch and support highly visible community campaigns. These included a Spirit of Vancouver campaign, a Symphony in the Park event, and trying to bring the 2010 Winter Olympics to Vancouver.

Did their plan work? Yes, it did, and in a big way. The Vancouver Board of Trade won the American Chamber of Commerce Executives' 2005 Award for Excellence. By 2007, membership revenues were up more than 50 percent, long-term member retention had improved to a record 95 percent, and membership had approached 5,000 for the first time.

The Spirit campaign and the Symphony in the Park program were successfully launched and Vancouver was awarded the 2010 Winter Olympic Games. To the casual observer, it probably all looked like magic. Of course it wasn't, though. All this success came out of having a strong sense of purpose that dovetailed with an ambitious but realistic plan for growth.

Mix It Up!

Be sure your purpose-driven plan is written, well communicated, and, as circumstances dictate, regularly updated. Consider the words of President Dwight Eisenhower, who once said, "Plans are useless, but planning is indispensable."

Chapter 15

You Gotta Serve Somebody

During the first half of the twentieth century, Dr. Wesley Wilkerson was an eye, ear, nose, and throat specialist practicing in Nashville, Tennessee. Throughout his early career, Dr. Wilkerson was frustrated by the lack of specialized services for the hearing-impaired children he treated in his community. He was especially concerned about the lack of skilled intervention at a young age to help these children with their communication skills later in life. He saw an important need, and by the 1930s he had taken it upon himself to fill it.

Sometime after Christmas 1944, Dr. Wilkerson's only son Bill also saw an important need and filled it. Officers asked for volunteers for the dangerous job of forward observer at the height of the Battle of the Bulge, Hitler's last-gasp attempt to turn the tide of World War II. More than 500,000 young American men fought in that four-week battle, and over 80,000 casualties were sustained—the bloodiest battle of the entire war. Bill raised his hand to help his country one day and paid the ultimate price. He was only 19 years old.

By 1949, Dr. Wilkerson had campaigned and cajoled enough support to form the Tennessee Hearing and Speech Foundation. Two years later, the foundation's board of directors agreed to open a care clinic in an old Vanderbilt University fraternity house. After asking Dr. Wilkerson to leave the room, the board also unanimously voted to name the new facility the Bill Wilkerson Hearing and Speech Center, in honor of the fallen hero.

As the father of a teenage boy, I'm guessing the hole in Dr. Wilkerson heart was too big to ever be filled completely. Nonetheless, the board saw a couple of real needs that day and sought to fill them. It must have been a proud moment for the good doctor and his family.

In 1978, Dr. Fred Bess became director of the expanding Bill Wilkerson Center. By the mid-1990s, under his guidance, it had grown to a staff of 80 dedicated professionals serving some 4,000 patients. Like any good growth leader would have, Dr. Bess began to sense that the demands of the community were increasing beyond the facility's capacity. He saw a need and looked to fill it. He sought, along with the board, to merge the private clinic with the Vanderbilt Medical Center. In 1997, the Vanderbilt Bill Wilkerson Center for Otolaryngology and Communication Sciences was formed.

Since the merger, the Center has doubled in size and scope. Eight thousand patients a year are helped by a staff of over 150 working across five different departments, whose services now range from helping preschoolers with communication disorders to aiding seniors with hearing loss. *U.S. News & World Report* rated the graduate program in audiology number one in the country. The community keeps coming to the Center with its needs, and the Center grows by filling those needs.

I first became familiar with the Center and its important work after meeting Lucy, the five-year-old daughter of friends. She had recently been diagnosed with a form of autism. She is a sweet and funny and loving child, but was unable to speak. This was profoundly frustrating for her parents and even more so for Lucy.

After only a few months of working with a Center specialist, dramatic improvements for Lucy were obvious to even this untrained observer. She quickly mastered a talker, an electronic gizmo about the size of a laptop that she presses to put together complex thoughts. I became the butt of more than one of her talker jokes (such as "I think you a crazy" after watching me unsuccessfully try to use the complex contraption).

A few weeks later, Lucy began to vocalize actual words. For her parents, it was a moment they had feared might never come. I can only imagine their elation at hearing those first halting but easily understood words: "B-oo-k. C-a-t. M-om-my. D-ad-dy." Lucy's parents had and will continue to have a true need, and the Center is there to fill it.

No matter what your organization endeavors to achieve, the lessons of the Vanderbilt Bill Wilkerson Center apply to you.

(The purpose of any organization is to identify and fill the relevant needs of those it serves.)

As a result of purpose-driven leadership, the Center stands as one shining example of how organizational growth happens. It begins, and is subsequently propelled by, what Helen Keller once called "fidelity to a worthy purpose."

Dr. Wilkerson never gave up on a need he identified as critical to the community he served. The board had an inspired, purposeful start and guided the Bill Wilkerson Center through decades of change and progress. Dr. Bess could have easily seen a merger with a larger institution as a threat to the autonomy the private facility had always enjoyed. Instead, risking even his own job, he pushed for the union that proved to be the right call for expanded patient care. Later, we will learn even more about Dr. Bess and his proven leadership skills.

I am looking forward to the day when I can tell an older Lucy the story of young Bill Wilkerson and his self-less sacrifice. I am anticipating she will respond with a perfectly enunciated "Good story, Steve . . . but you are still full of p-oo-p."

Mix It Up!

Find ways to keep the needs of those you serve at the top of everyone's priority list. If an action item doesn't directly relate to this, question why it's an item at all.

(Extra Toppings)

Reconfirm that your organization has a unique purpose

If you don't have a unique purpose, I suggest you create one ASAP. If you do have one, then be sure it is truly unique, credible, and capable of getting people out of bed in the morning.

Frequently articulate your organization's stated purpose

In the heat of battle, it's easy for troops to lose sight of what they are fighting for. It's the job of a leader to remind everyone that their struggle serves a higher calling. To that end, your unique purpose should be both clear and concise.

Stand up and make a difference

"Going along to get along" is no way to grow. Do the right thing, even when the stupid systems appear to be stacked against you.

Section 4
Insource Crucial
Judgment

Much has been written and discussed regarding the out-sourcing movement taking place in today's organizations. For many, the word *outsource* conjures up an image of a teleworker in a developing nation struggling to sound authentic in a second language. For others, the idea is a log-ical, cost-saving measure that helps ensure global competi-tiveness. I suppose both notions are based on reality.

For me, there is no right or wrong when it comes to outsourcing. Outsourcing a payroll function to payroll experts, for instance, has made sense for many organiza-tions for years. If it make sense to outsource a payroll process domestically, can't it also be possible to do it with a foreign provider?

Toyota's highly successful Lexus brand routinely out-sources vehicle design in its "relentless pursuit of perfec-tion," but consciously "insources" the assembly process. I'm less concerned with outsourcing than I am with insourc-ing. Whenever an organizational leader consciously decides which crucial judgments should be kept internal, that's insourcing.

Today's growth leaders hone their judgment skills when deciding what to keep in and what to send out. Ultimately, this honing of judgment leads to wisdom. Leaders also tap into the collective wisdom of those who work with and for them in order to build organizations that are positioned to identify and fill changing needs.

Chapter 16

Edicts Made on High

Everybody seems to know what the term *catch-22* means. While they may not know its derivation, they understand it to be a circular, conflicting set of rules descending from a nameless, faceless bureaucracy. Anyone who has spent any time in any organization of any size has experienced the phenomenon.

Joseph Heller's *Catch-22* was published in 1961 and has come to define our understanding that organizations are often absurd, especially for the individual caught in an organization's cogs. The now-classic novel is set in the waning days of World War II and illustrates the concept of circular logic. In an attempt to be excused from dangerous duty, a bombardier seeks to get a doctor's diagnosis that he is insane. Yet regulations assume that only a sane person would recognize the inherent danger of the mission. By requesting leave from duty on the grounds of insanity, the bombardier actually proves that he is sane and therefore fit to fly.

While you may not be dealing with life and death and questions of sanity versus insanity, we all recognize

103

the no-win situation (damned if I do, damned if I don't) paradox. For most of us, it starts in school. For instance, in order to gain admission to a better college, we need to have good grades and strong participation in extracurricular activities. Yet being in the marching band and chess club actually takes time away from our studies.

Once we are flung out of our educational systems, we face the equally perplexing "You must have experience to get a job, but you can't get a job without experience" dilemma.

Once you get that first job, it only becomes worse. I can remember the first time I experienced it as a young manager in advertising. I was asked during a period of downsizing to fire one of the three younger people reporting to me. Two of these young people were all-stars, while one was barely making it. Yet we fired one of the all-stars because the laggard had cost the organization more money. You see, neither of the all-stars had an advanced degree, while the laggard possessed a master's degree. There had been a hiring bonus, a substantial investment in training, and an extra $10,000 a year in salary.

The organization had too much invested in the underperformer. Managers many levels above me had to make it work in order to save face. Despite my best efforts, I was faced with the moral quandary of firing an overachiever in order to keep an underachiever. Within six months, I was out of advertising forever.

Just recently, I made a reservation to stay at a Disney property in Orlando, Florida. I had been asked to speak at an event, and this hotel was perfectly located for me. I called the systemwide reservation number and was assisted by a gentleman who could not have been more pleasant. Everything went swimmingly until the very end. I made what I thought to be a very simple request: "Could you send me a confirmation by e-mail, please?"

That request was greeted with, "I'm sorry, sir, we don't e-mail confirmations anymore. We will, however, be mailing you all the information you need very soon."

Mailing a confirmation probably works for most of the company's hotel's customers. However, it was peak business travel season for me. I wouldn't be anywhere near my mailbox in order to intercept the paper-based confirmation.

I explained to the cheery "cast member" that I really needed the confirmation e-mailed because I was on the road. The Cast Member replied that because customers tended to lose their e-mail confirmations due to spam filters and operator error, he was no longer authorized to e-mail the information. It was for my own good.

Ten minutes later I was still trying to explain that I somewhat understood his argument. However, he really needed to understand mine. The Disney hotel properties used to e-mail confirmations, and every other hotel chain

Edicts Made on High

I do business with can send me an e-mail confirmation. Also, sending it by e-mail would have represented an incremental cost to Disney of zippo. Zilch. Nada!

Throughout our good-natured back-and-forth, I couldn't help but think to myself, "Hey, Goofy, you can snail-mail the damn thing anywhere you want. Just send me an e-mail, too!"

The Disney brand is synonymous with service. Anyone who has stayed at one of its hotels or visited one of its parks knows that nobody does the details better. However, in this instance, I never did get the e-mail confirmation I requested. (I did find the snail-mail confirmation stacked on my desk a couple of weeks after my stay.) I was so intrigued by this pointless policy that I couldn't let it go.

After numerous phone calls to the organization trying to better understand it all, I eventually ended up with a particularly perky PR person at headquarters in Anaheim, California. The circular nature of our conversation would have no doubt brought a smile to Joseph Heller's face. I had hit the bureaucratic wall.

To this day, I don't think she completely believed what she was telling me. She did, however, believe in Disney's infallibility. It was as if she were saying, "I don't know whether it makes sense. What I do know is the House of

Mouse has decreed it, and therefore, by definition, it is correct."

Any attempts at logic (such as I'm on the road right now and won't be home in time to get it, I know you used to do it, it won't cost you anything extra to do it, all other hotels can do it) were met with the canned response, "Yes, but I was told that people lose them. It's really better for you if we mail it." Eventually I gave up.

In my first book I described a very similar situation with my carrier of choice, Delta Air Lines. While the marketing department was able to send me e-mails on a weekly basis, the reservation system didn't know my e-mail address. In this case, they were more than happy to send me an e-mail confirmation; they just didn't have my e-mail address. How is that possible? How could the left hand of the organization know my e-mail address, yet the right hand was forced to reinvent the wheel every time? When the book was published in 2005, I honestly believed this situation would soon be resolved. I am sorry to report that as of 2008, the stupid system remains unchanged.

When rules, policies, and procedures are made at the highest levels, it's those at the bottom who usually suffer— sometimes to an extreme degree. A Wendy's employee was shot by an angry customer after refusing to give the customer more than three packets of chili sauce—the corporate policy–mandated limit.

107

Home Depot recently fired a manager and former Employee of the Year for thwarting an attempted robbery. A spokesperson for Home Depot cited "safety" and "company policy" as the justifications. I'm willing to bet the fear of litigation in the executive suites might have had more to do with it.

Major record labels continue to sue their most ardent fans for illegal downloading. While protecting intellectual property is complicated, I can't imagine that suing teenagers for sharing music is an effective growth strategy.

Policies become pointless when senior officials far from the front lines mandate edicts from on high. The policies may appear logical, but eventually these remotely made mandates don't fit the realities of the situations. The companies have insourced the policy function, but they keep it in the hands of managers who are the least likely to make it actually work.

Mix It Up!

Break the catch-22 cycle by questioning hierarchical mandates. You simply can't mix a milkshake from an executive suite.

Chapter 17

Peeves from Below

For many years now, I've been telling the story of Stuart and the elusive milkshake. Despite my best efforts to impress upon an audience or an individual that the lesson of the milkshake lies in stupid systems, too often people try to bring it back to the hapless Stuart. "Stuart isn't empowered," they say. Isn't it interesting how these buzzwords seep into organization-speak everywhere? I'm not sure who first said it, but "empower your employees" has been a mantra for well over a decade now.

There's no question that pushing certain decisions down to the point of contact is a very good idea in a wide range of situations, including customer service, vendor relations, and various forms of process improvement. So let me be clear from the start that I am in favor of empowered employees in a broad array of circumstances.

However, penning policy is not one of them. Just as organizations are vulnerable to pointless policies when constructed at the highest levels, rogue individuals far from the executive suites are also common perpetrators of senseless rules and procedures.

Here's an example. Recently I suffered with my yearly bout of swimmer's ear. After visiting the doctor, I went straight to my regular pharmacy chain, with an official prescription in hand. It was midday and things were rather slow. Although no one was in line at the pharmacist's counter, it took her a few minutes to acknowledge my presence. At first I was a bit perturbed at the wait, but in retrospect I'm glad I had a few minutes to look around. My eye was eventually drawn to this:

> **To our customers:**
> **We do not interrupt cellular phone calls!**
> **Please finish your conversation before stepping up to the counter for service.**
> **Thank you.**

On the surface the statement "We do not interrupt cellular phone calls" seems polite. Isn't that nice of them? They don't want to interrupt me. But wait a minute, is that an exclamation point? Yes, it is. Do you know what that means? They are, in effect, yelling at me—subtly perhaps, but they're yelling all the same. They might even be cursing.

This laminated 8½ × 11 inch sign told me a lot about this place. The sign was obviously created on someone's

PC and had the telltale signs of a clip art template spit out of a $99 inkjet printer. Clearly someone had created this at home. My first reaction was one of feeling chastised. I hadn't even spoken to the pharmacist yet, and already I was being preemptively accused of something I didn't do.

I had become relegated to that needy, impolite class of people known as "customers." This was not my first time in this particular pharmacy, and I had always found it to be a smoothly running operation. It had earned my loyalty up to this point, which was probably why I was standing there, willing to wait. Eventually the pharmacist emerged from the well-stocked shelves and asked, in a polite voice, "How may I help you?" Most people would have simply handed her the prescription, but I guess I'm not like most people. I couldn't let this one go, either.

I said, "Yes, you can help me. I'm writing a book on policies. Can you tell me more about this one?" I picked up the offending laminate and held it close to my smiling face.

Now, quite honestly, I assumed that the sign had been created by someone else, probably an assistant manager or an easily bothered cashier. What pharmacist would take the time to create something like this? As it turned out, my assumption could not have been more wrong. After she processed my question, her polite smile quickly changed to a defensive scowl. She didn't have to say a word. I now knew who had created the sign.

111

Fannie the Pharmacist (not her real name, by the way) proceeded to give me a seemingly bullet-pointed list of all the reasons why this policy made sense. She invoked Health Insurance Portability and Accountability Act (HIPAA) regulations. Clearer communications. Courtesy for others waiting in line. Expediency. In her mind, the argument was sealed tighter than a childproof cap.

I listened for as long as Fannie wanted to vent. Then it was my turn. I asked, "How often does this really happen? What if it's truly an emergency and I'm on the phone with the prescribing doctor or my ailing family member? Is this a chainwide policy?" She managed to avoid directly answering any of my specific questions and instead returned to her tired talking points. I tried to press further, but it soon became clear that this was very personal to her. Besides, my ear hurt. I took my drops and left.

Since that day, I've been to other locations of this pharmacy chain and those of its competitors. I've yet to see another sign like it. I've also talked to a number of pharmacists about the sign, and, excluding Fannie, I was able to draw a general consensus. Fannie's sign represented a pet peeve, not a pertinent policy. While they all agreed that a customer cell phone call is an occasional nuisance, it wasn't anywhere near the top of their list of significant problems.

While I'll never know for sure, I'm willing to bet a summer's supply of eardrops that Fannie's sign was born of frustration. She is frustrated that she went to pharmacy school for years, yet, due to cutbacks, is forced to serve in a dual role as both pharmacist and cashier. She is frustrated that people don't treat her with the respect she feels a professional deserves. Fannie is taking her frustration out on everybody with her pointless policy power play.

Am I reading too much into all this? Maybe. I am even willing to concede that cell phones could possibly create some problems now and again. But here's my point: This issue is simply not worthy of a sign, let alone an exclamation point. If every empowered employee were to put up signs representing their individual pet peeves, our offices, work sites, warehouses, and stores would be littered with the physical manifestations of every individual's annoyances.

If you're going to allow a sign on cell phone usage, what's going to stop the posting of signs like these?

To our customers:
We will not abide talking or whining children!
Please lock them in the car before approaching the counter.
Thank you.

> To our customers:
> Please, no loud gum chewing while
> standing in line!
> It's distracting!
> Thank you.

> To our customers:
> We will not interrupt your coffee drinking!
> Please dispose of your babble-inducing
> lattes in the proper trash receptacles.
> Thank you.

> To our customers:
> Please perfect your debit card swiping skills
> on your own time before approaching our
> counter!
> It is not our job to teach you.
> Thank you.

Ridiculous? Absolutely, but really no more ridiculous than Fanny's sign.

Mix It Up!

Discern between positive initiatives and rogue individualism. Insourcing crucial judgment does not mean entertaining everyone's pet peeve.

Chapter 18

Participatory Policy Making

In Chapter 15 we learned about the purpose-driven growth of the Vanderbilt Bill Wilkerson Center. Since 1978, Dr. Fred Bess has been the Center's leader. You may remember that he was one of the individuals who was instrumental in merging the then private Bill Wilkerson Center with Vanderbilt University's medical center in 1997. One hundred percent growth was the result.

What I didn't explain is that by merging the two organizations, Dr. Bess had in effect agreed to a title change from "Director" to "Associate Director." His function didn't change, mind you, but his title did. But real growth leaders don't need titles to get the job done.

I have never met Dr. Bess. Instead, I have spoken to many who work with and for him. To a person, they tell the story of a remarkably accomplished man who leads the way people want to be led.

"He has a knack for knowing when something needs to change in order for us to move forward and grow," said one who has worked with him for 20 years. (I heard, "He's timely.") Another told me, "In order to be able to take advantage of the changes happening around us, we needed to join forces with a larger entity." (I heard, "He's realistic.") A PR professional at the Center described him as "lovably idiosyncratic." (That sounded like "unscripted" to my ears.) "He has a good feel for the emotions of different people." (That is the perfect definition of how I would use *sensitive* when describing a growth leader.)

After having continued to raise funds for the Center as a private entity, he offered to return any monies collected once the merger with Vanderbilt University began to unfold. In his mind, the Center always needed to be transparent when dealing with the outside world. One patron said she probably would have asked for her donation back had Dr. Bess not personally visited her to explain the entire situation. Over the years, everyone has come to TRUST Dr. Fred Bess.

One of the most intriguing ways in which Dr. Bess fosters Milkshake Moments can be seen in the Center's policy toward policies. Let me explain.

The Center is now made up of five different divisions that offer treatment for a wide range of conditions that affect hearing, speech, language, and voice production. The Voice Center, the Pediatric Feeding and Swallowing Program, and the Augmentative Communication Program are just a few of the Center's programs that draw patients from across the state and region. While there is some commonality for all the departments, there are also many differences.

Anyone from a senior citizen recovering from larynx cancer to a preschool child with a cleft palate is regularly served by the Center. As a result, policies that relate to patients create some special challenges. What is the policy on spouses in the room during treatment? Who can take a child on a bathroom break? Can siblings be in the room during sessions? If yes, how old must they be? If no, are they allowed to play alone in the waiting area while the parent attends the treatment? How many people should man the phones at any given time?

In most organizations, these types of challenges would be remedied in the way we've already seen earlier. The big, general stuff would be handled on high by people the furthest removed from the actual situation. The specific stuff would be pushed down to individuals who might not be able to see the unintended consequences of their policy actions. Of course, the Vanderbilt Bill Wilkerson Center isn't typical of most organizations, and Dr. Bess is a Milkshake Moment maven.

At the Center, each division has a policy-making committee. How this committee is formed is left to the discretion of the heads of each division, thanks to Dr. Bess

117

demonstrating full trust in his direct reports. While each division has a different committee makeup, they all share the notion that it should represent a broad cross section of the division in terms of age, tenure, position, etc.

They also share a "we meet whenever we need to meet" policy. Instead of quarterly or every third Thursday, they meet when one committee member gets a couple of others to agree that they need to meet. And these meetings are usually short—typically one hour maximum. If something can't get decided in that hour, they move on. If an idea is tabled or rejected, that doesn't mean it can't be revisited later.

Policy-making responsibilities for the committees now range from patient care issues to length of lunch breaks. And while there are certainly some University policies to which they all must adhere, Dr. Bess has created an environment in which his staff has a big say in things that matter most.

Mix It Up!

Trust that teams can mix their own policy milkshakes and know that homemade ones are always the easiest to swallow.

Chapter 19

How 'bout Them Pomegranates?

Until just a few years ago, I didn't know the difference between a pomegranate and a Pomeranian. Thanks to one focused growth leader, however, I now know more about the versatile pomegranate than almost any other fruit. And it has all happened so fast.

Somehow I've gone from never seeing or hearing about a pomegranate to having it pop up on every menu, in every grocery store aisle, and in every convenience store in the United States: pomegranate Popsicles, pomegranate margaritas, pomegranate glazed pork chops, pomegranate infused sea bass. Unless you've had your head buried in an apple orchard, I'm sure you've noticed the emergence of this new "superfruit."

Yep, we already had superpowers, superstars, supermodels, and Super Bowls. Now we have superfruits. The pomegranate used to be an obscure fruit that only 12 percent of the American public knew about and only 4 percent had ever tasted. Now it has pushed its way to the top of the fruit pile and has achieved superfruit status. Where was the fig when all this happened? It took blueberries a hundred years to work their way up to superfruit status, and then the pomegranate cut to the front of the line. They have now become the Beatles of the produce world. Pomegranatemania is upon us.

How did this happen?

For a road warrior like me who spends a lot of time in restaurants, it's glaringly apparent that food has become fashion and produce is now food's haute couture. From shiitake mushrooms to heirloom tomatoes, baby arugula to fingerling potatoes, produce moves from our fine dining menus to our frozen Lean Cuisine dinners. Today's designer produce eventually becomes tomorrow's grocery aisle staple.

So it has gone with the pomegranate. The sudden growth of this unlikely fruit—cultivated since ancient times throughout the Mediterranean—is a truly remarkable story. My curiosity got the best of me. This kind of growth, I thought to myself, doesn't happen without a Milkshake Moment.

My hunch proved correct. After digging a bit, I came to learn that a wealthy couple in California with a proven track record in growing businesses invested in some orchard land that was full of various fruits, including pomegranates.

Experts advised them to plow under the pomegranate trees and plant nuts instead.

Lynda Resnick thought it was the experts who were nuts. She loved not only the taste of the pomegranate, but the lore and the legend surrounding this exotic fruit. Resnick had also heard that the juice of the pomegranate had exceptional health benefits. She set out to prove it, in a big way, spending millions of dollars funding scientific studies on its properties.

And it worked. POM Wonderful juices were introduced to the U.S. market in 2002, and, while the company is still privately held, worldwide annual sales are purported to be well over $100 million. The vast majority of the U.S. strain of pomegranates is grown in one valley in California. The Resnicks now control the majority of that supply. This has allowed them not only to grow their own bottled juice brand, but to garner a portion of the revenue generated from the 478 new pomegranate products introduced by other companies in the United States in 2006 alone.

Wow! Unbelievable! In only five years they've created a category that didn't exist before and turned this underdog fruit into a phenomenon. What's most interesting to me as a growth expert is that this came from outside the industry. How did the managers working within the $700 billion global beverage marketplace allow an outsider to

How 'bout Them Pomegranates?

create and corner an entirely new juice category? I liken the pomegranate to the formerly plain Jane or John who struts into your high school reunion, turning heads and dropping jaws around the room. "Whoa, would you look at that? How did we not see all that potential?"

The lesson of the pomegranate is simple yet powerful. Pomegranate properties have not changed in thousands of years. The taste, the appearance, and the supposed medicinal properties have remained consistent. Yet it took one visionary David to slingshot the pomegranate right between the eyes of the beverage Goliaths. While other managers in that industry were busying themselves trying to move a soda drink from one calorie to zero and forcing calcium and high-fructose corn syrup into something approximating juice, Lynda Resnick and POM Wonderful, LLC relied on their inner judgment and single-handedly made the pomegranate ubiquitous.

This is a theme that's common to any organized human endeavor. The powerful yet myopic incumbents are often usurped by outsiders who don't know the rules well enough to even know they're breaking them. In my experience, substantive change regularly comes from these peripheral innovators. Indeed, this is not the first time it has happened in the beverage industry.

Coca-Cola, the world's largest beverage entity, recently paid $4.2 billion in cash (that's right, billion with a *b*) for

New York–based Glacéau, maker of brands like Vitamin Water and SmartWater. That's not a bad selling price for a company with previous-year earnings of only $350 million. Following the buyout, the *New York Times* quoted industry consultant Tom Pirko as saying, "When you look at what's happening with Coke, they can't innovate their way out. They have to buy their way out." (By the way, one of the best-selling flavors of VitaminWater is XXX, which includes—you guessed it—pomegranate juice.)

Lynda Resnick trusted her own judgment about their newly acquired orchards, and didn't follow the advice of the nutty experts. While POM Wonderful does outsource for advice on everything from packaging to production, one leader had the confidence to insource crucial judgment, and the subsequent success speaks for itself.

Lynda Resnick is a real grower. Don't be surprised if she doesn't soon find a way to deliver a pomegranate milkshake to a store near you.

Mix It Up!

Listen to your inner voice. Growth leaders learn that believing in their instincts can often bear the sweetest fruit.

Chapter 20

Come Harter or High Water

There are always challenges related to growth. If it were easy, everyone would be doing it. When it comes to growth, what you can count on is not being able to count on anything. In fact, rarely can growth be traced back to simply actions taken during good times. More often than not, it has as much to do with how a leader reacts to adversity as opportunity. Opportunities are usually pretty apparent. True adversity makes self-doubters of us all.

Think you've seen some tough times? Consider the story of Michael Harter and the team at Intoprint Technologies.

In 1989, Michael Harter and Frank Hill started a Virginia-based distributor of products for commercial printers. By 2003 sales were going well and had reached several million dollars, so they decided to expand by acquiring a distributor with a similar product mix. The purchase would extend their territory further south into the Gulf Coast region. By combining the two businesses, they would strengthen sales synergy, with some 70 percent of their products supplied by one of the best-known brands in the

125

business. The future looked very bright to our friends at Intoprint. But looks can be deceiving. The unexpected was about to come pounding on their door.

On March 31, 2004, Intoprint closed on a substantial bank loan in order to purchase the other distributorship. Three and a half months later, the primary supplier to both businesses filed for bankruptcy. Immediately they noticed problems with deliveries. The partners were concerned. But the ordeal had just begun.

On September 6, 2004, the first of four major hurricanes hit the newly acquired Gulf Coast territory. Each hurricane brought unique trials and tribulations for Harter and his crew. Telecommunications for the entire business were centered in Mobile, Alabama. Even without a direct hit, the internal and external communications systems would be down for days on end. Employee attendance was spotty, as many families suffered significant damage or even total losses of their homes. The supply chain became even less reliable. Print runs moved to other parts of the country, lowering demand from their customers.

As we all remember, once hurricanes Katrina and Rita hit within a month of each other, gasoline prices quickly spiked and stayed high. For any distribution and on-site servicing business, transportation is one of the primary variable costs. Meanwhile, the loan Intoprint took out in March of 2004 was tied to the prime rate. Interest rates

The Milkshake Moment

rose nationally, climbing from 4.75 percent to 9.25 percent, essentially doubling the loan payments—at a time Intoprint could least afford it. Some pretty dark clouds were now obscuring the once-bright future.

Any one of these setbacks could have caused the average leader to throw up his or her hands and say, "Oh, well, bad luck. Not my fault. Nothing I can do now." But Michael Harter and his team are not ordinary leaders.

They quickly identified those areas that needed immediate attention. First, they knew they needed to flip their revenue mix. In other words, they rightly decided to significantly decrease their dependency on the bankrupt supplier. Second, they determined that the only way they could achieve this type of turnaround was through their people. "Eventually, I had a pretty good idea of what we needed to do," said Michael. "The question in my mind was whether or not we could convince our staff of what we needed to do."

The key to the turnaround was clearly getting both the old sales force and the new sales force to embrace the new revenue flip. Some got it right away. Others took some time. In the end, a few didn't make it. For those who did, trust was a core factor. Through the team's timely decision making, realistic goal setting, unscripted communication, sensitivity to individual needs, and an openly transparent style, Intoprint not only survived, but thrived.

127

Despite being rocked by seemingly one catastrophe after another, Michael and his partners never felt sorry for themselves. Given the string of setbacks, it would have been reasonable for any leaders to question their judgment. I'm sure there were more than a few tough days. Yet by not allowing the winds of adversity to throw them off their charted course, Intoprint sailed on to growth.

I've always maintained that a privately held, sustained growth organization is one that can achieve growth of 20 percent or greater five years in a row. Despite Intoprint's incredible obstacles, it is about to close the books on its third year of 20 percent or more growth. In only five years, sales have more than tripled and the business has grown to 41 loyal employees.

After hearing Michael tell his story, I have no doubt that he will become a member of that exclusive club of proven sustained growth leaders. Forced into a daily crash course on good judgment, Michael Harter and Intoprint have realized not only real growth, but true wisdom.

Mix It Up!

Hone your judgment skills through experience to enhance your wisdom, and thereby grow your organization. In the face of adversity, wisdom usually wins.

Extra Toppings

Don't allow phrases like these to go unchallenged
Clichés like the following could very well be true. They could also be an unnecessary hindrance to growth. You need to be the judge.

"Our consultant told us it was the next big thing."
"Our accountant made us do it to save money."
"Our lawyers said we had to or else we could get sued."
"We don't need to reinvent the wheel on this one."
"Information Technology (IT) says it would be a big mistake to do it that way."
"We tried that once; it doesn't work in this kind of organization."

Policy manuals tend to gather dust
For a policy system to truly work it must be consistently reviewed and reinforced, be representative, and be regularly communicated.

Consider that leaders are readers and readers are leaders
The wiser we become, the better decisions we make. The better decisions we make, the more likely it is our organizations will grow. The more our organizations grow, the more able we are to attract great people who can do

great things. That allows us to spend more time reading, listening, and gaining wisdom. See how that works?

People often ask me for a list of books they should read. Let me first say that I am a big fan of magazines and suggest reading a couple every day. However, when it comes to books, I find that histories and biographies teach us more about growth and change and the human condition than almost any management book. Here are a few books that I believe will help anyone with their growth aspirations:

Undaunted Courage: Meriwether Lewis, Thomas Jefferson, and the Opening of the American West, by Stephen E. Ambrose (Simon & Schuster, 1997).
The Effective Executive: The Definitive Guide to Getting the Right Things Done, by Peter F. Drucker (Harper & Row, 1967).
Made to Stick: Why Some Ideas Survive and Others Die, by Chip Heath and Dan Heath (Random House, 2007).
The Rise of Theodore Roosevelt, by Edmund Morris (Coward, McCann & Geoghegan, 1979).
The Rise and Fall of the Third Reich, by William L. Shirer (Simon & Schuster, 1960).

Section 5
Address the "People Problem" Problem

I talk to a lot of business growth leaders, including entrepreneurs at start-ups, managing directors of trade associations, and heads of global operations breaking into new markets. Nearly every time, they tell me their number-one obstacle to growth is the lack of great people. What's holding them back is not a capital access issue, market conditions, or government regulations. It's people. The smart leaders are confronting this issue with a variety of Milkshake Moments, putting their innovative energies into hiring, training, and retaining the very best.

Then there's everyone else.

When the OPEN division of American Express polled 625 business owners on what skills they would most like to develop further, what percentage answered "finding and retaining the best and brightest"? I don't know the answer, because people issues didn't make the top five. Instead, these owners mentioned the following areas:

1. Customer service
2. Marketing and sales
3. Financial management
4. Decision making
5. Negotiation

The greatest barrier to growth for most organizations is the people problem, and everyone knows it—but little is done to even acknowledge it, let alone solve it.

Therein lies the problem. Finding and keeping the best and brightest is a clear competitive advantage, but too few would-be growth leaders are willing to make it a priority. Why? It all gets back to what I said in Section 2: Most managers get up and do what they want to do, not what needs to be done. Quite simply, most people don't enjoy working on people issues.

Do you see the opportunity here? Organizations that are growing give hiring, training, and retaining the emphasis they deserve. Many managers of organizations that aren't growing concentrate on everything *but* the people problem problem, then are the first to complain that they "just can't find good help anymore."

Next time you hear someone bad-mouth the American work ethic, please consider:

- While the number of hours worked per week is decreasing in every other industrialized country, in the United States the average worker is toiling more hours per week than he or she did 25 years ago, according to the Bureau of Labor Statistics.

- In a Yahoo! Hot Jobs survey, 45 percent of respondents did not take all of their vacation days in the previous year, while 39 percent said they were too exhausted to take a real vacation. The number-one reason for not taking their allotted time? "Too much work."

Address the "People Problem" Problem

- According to the *Wall Street Journal*, the average CEO now gets paid more than $400 for every $1 earned by the average worker. In 1990 CEO pay was less than $150 for the average worker's $1.

- Nearly half of all private-sector workers get no paid sick days, says the *New York Times*. For food service workers, it's 86 percent. (How 'bout a sneeze with those fries, ma'am?)

The U.S. Bureau of Labor Statistics estimates a shortage of skilled workers of 10 million by 2010 and as many as 35 million within the next 30 years. Our growing economy, retiring baby boomers, and a shift to an information- and service-based economy are all contributing to the crisis.

There's an escalating war for talent, and it's only going to get worse. We can quibble over projections and statistical methods and immigration trends, but those are issues around the margins. A recent survey of 4,000 hiring managers covered in the *Economist* magazine found that the time to fill a vacancy had grown from 37 days in 2004 to 51 days just three years later. Of the managers surveyed, 62 percent worried about company-wide talent shortages and more than a third admitted to hiring below-average candidates "just to fill a position." Don't count on the "people problem" problem to get solved here or anywhere else in the Western world anytime soon. This is one area screaming for some Milkshake Moments.

Chapter 21

The People Problem Polka

I recently did some work for one of the world's leaders in data storage products. The California-based company has grown at a tremendous rate, due in large measure to market conditions. Everything from Sarbanes-Oxley requirements to health information protection mandated by the Health Insurance Portability and Accountability Act (HIPAA) has made data storage security more important than ever. That's just the beginning. The need to store data has moved far beyond the traditional health, legal, and financial industries. Secure and readily accessible information is now a core requirement for nearly every organization.

This company has grown faster than the overall market by partnering with a series of value-added resellers. These independently owned information technology specialists offer a wide range of IT solutions, including data security. For the past several years, they have all grown very well together.

This particular data storage company hosted a series of three two-day learning events for their most valuable partners (MVPs). So, just to review, what we have here is a really fast-growing, well-run data storage company conducting learning events for their fast-growing, well-run partners. So far, so good.

I was the only outside observer invited to these events. Therefore, I could offer nothing but an outsider's perspective. What I heard at all three events was very consistent. The data storage company did a tremendous job of explaining their new products, policies, and processes. Discussions at the lunch tables and over beers at night invariably sounded like a popular song with familiar words. It had the merchandise melody and the bells and whistles accompaniment, backed by the channel conflict chorus—typical battle hymns, straight from the trenches, sung by those fighting in the field.

Regardless of endeavor, when you put the leaders of partnering organizations together, they sing about "the thing." "The thing" is their perception of what they do. In this case, they sell black boxes. Therefore, they like to sing songs about black boxes. They like to sing songs about selling black boxes. They like to sing songs about the people who buy black boxes. And every bit of this is productive and necessary. The outsider approved.

But this outsider always looks for errors of omission. For me, it's like seeing my favorite band in concert. I like all the songs they're playing, but I am disappointed if

I don't hear my favorite. While I enjoyed the entire set list for these events, my favorite song was missing: "The People Problem Polka."

The funny thing is, it took an outsider to recognize the missing song. The whole purpose of these events was for the solution provider to help its reseller network grow, thereby growing along with the resellers. At all three events, I asked the resellers the same question I ask every group of leaders: "What is your biggest barrier to growth?"

They sang "Resources!" in perfect harmony. *Resources*, I've come to learn, is the IT industry's word for *people*. Usually, in organization-speak, the word *resources* refers to raw materials or capital, not people. When they said that *resources* meant human beings, it got my attention.

What got my attention even more, however, was that while everyone agreed that resources were indeed the biggest barrier to growth, they spent their two-day hootenanny singing the same song they always sing: "The Ballad of the Black Box."

Boy, they love that song, and they sure are good at singing it. They can't get enough of it. And it's a good song! Tales of intrigue and heroism, booms and busts, comedy and tragedy, conflict and resolution. It's their "Stairway to Freebird."

Why do they keep practicing the song they know so well when they've already identified the "The People Problem Polka" as the one song needing the most attention? This group never rehearsed it once. They love that "Ballad of the Black Box" so much that they keep adding verses. If you're over 40 years of age, think Don McLean's "American Pie." If you're under 40, think R. Kelly's "In the Closet."

Please don't misunderstand me. This is one of my favorite groups. By anyone's measure, these guys are number one in their genre. But my job was to suggest how to keep this current supergroup from becoming tomorrow's has-beens. The tune that they needed to work on the most was obvious to me and apparently not unknown to them. Like so many of us, however, they had chosen to keep playing the same old tune they know so well.

Mix It Up!

Listen for tired tunes in your organization. Are you playing them to death? Maybe it's time to rock "The People Problem Polka."

Chapter 22

Eric's Excalibur

I meet admirable people almost every day: business leaders, community activists, single parents working two jobs just to make ends meet. None of them ever considers themselves to be a hero. Such is the case with Eric Hoover.

In early 2006, the Meadville, Pennsylvania, Chamber of Commerce asked me to be the keynote speaker at their annual dinner. Hundreds of outstanding people were there that evening. One definitely stood out. Just before taking the stage, I was introduced to Eric, who had just been named National Small Businessperson of the Year by the Small Business Administration in Washington, D.C. (By the way, the second-place finisher was Andrew Field, founder of PrintingForLess.com, about whom I wrote extensively in my first book.)

Eric was asked to say a few words to the audience before I spoke, and he politely agreed. However, it was obvious that he was uncomfortable tooting his own horn.

The local official introducing him reeled off a list of accomplishments that got my undivided attention. Eric's humble aw-shucks demeanor really piqued my curiosity. Hearing him speak, I made a mental note that this man had an even bigger story to tell.

At the end of the evening I approached Eric and asked if I might one day come back to visit him. He said, "Sure, that would be great." He probably thought that was the last he would ever hear of me. Instead, a few months later he was gracious enough to allow me to visit with him for a day. I traveled to Conneaut Lake, Pennsylvania (population 700), seven miles from the sprawling metropolis of Meadville (population 13,421).

Eric Hoover founded the Excalibur Machine Co. Inc., a metal fabrication business, in 1988, while holding down a full-time manufacturing job. Ten years later he made the leap to running Excalibur full-time. That's when things got really interesting. Sales grew by more than 350 percent and he was employing 125 people by the time he won this prestigious award.

Over the course of our day together it began to dawn on me that I was in the presence of a truly gifted leader. Reserved to the point of being shy, Eric was more of a shower than a teller. He showed me his original 7,000-square-foot facility. He showed me his new 30,000-square-foot

The Milkshake Moment

plant. He then drove me to a host of other community projects in which he was involved. It wasn't until we sat down for lunch that I got to hear the story behind the success.

The secret to Eric Hoover's success is so simple yet so profound. Eric built his business in order to serve his community and the people who lived within it. His growth story fascinated me. He started out making very large custom machine tool parts when the machine tool industry was supposedly dying in this country. Where most people saw decline, he saw opportunity. And he didn't stop there.

After shipping these large parts around the country for some time, Eric began to notice problems with the standard pallets he was using. His heavy parts were ripping them to shreds, and it was costing him real money. "No problem," he thought. "We'll just make our own." He contacted two acquaintances who had recently been downsized from their woodworking jobs. In no time, Excalibur not only was making its own heavy-duty pallets, but was marketing them to others in the region with a similar need. A new business was born.

Once the pallet business reached critical mass, the two original woodworkers approached Eric with another idea. They wanted to get back into custom cabinetry, their

Eric's Excalibur

true passion. Somehow that move into custom cabinetry led Eric Hoover and his passionate woodworkers into Lancelot Construction, builders of fine homes.

Similar to his pallet opportunity, Eric experienced problems with both cost and delivery from his trucking vendors. Blade Transport is now a separate profit center hauling goods for Excalibur and its partners for a fraction of the old cost. One of the drivers for Blade had earlier suffered a back injury while working for another trucking firm. After fully recuperating, he was still laid off. "I'm just looking for another chance," he told Eric. That driver has been on the road successfully for Blade Transport now for three years.

Eric Hoover understands people. Another proven leader in the community was unhappy in his long-term position as general sales manager at a local auto dealer. Eric said, "Come work for me."

"Doing what?" asked the wary sales manager.

"I want you to sell our machine tooling services," he replied.

"I don't know anything about machined parts, Eric."

"That's all right," Eric said. "If you can sell cars, you can sell our services."

"But I love cars. Cars are my life," the sales manager said.

The solution was so obvious, yet I'm confident I wouldn't have come up with it, and I doubt most other so-called leaders would have, either. Eric Hoover believes in people. He invests in other people's passions.

His solution was to hire the former sales manager for Excalibur, and at the same time he founded Zeljak Auto Sales, a seller of late-model used cars. You have to see it to believe it. We pulled off of a well-trafficked rural pike into a used car lot, where we were greeted by the woman who handles tags, titles, taxes, and the like. You walk through the car lot office and lo and behold, there's a state-of-the-art machine tool facility, with services sold by the same guy who is equally passionate about "his" new car lot.

(In a 2007 survey conducted by Yankelovich Partners, two-thirds of respondents said, "It is important that people see me as passionate about things that I care about.")

"Eric cares about this community," says my friend Charlie Anderson, president of the Meadville Chamber of Commerce and another formidable character. "He finds out what people are passionate about and then he funds it.

Everybody wins in that equation." I couldn't have said it better myself, Charlie.

Eric didn't let some national award go to his head. He's still driven by his purpose: helping his community, helping his neighbors, creating economic opportunities. In 2006 he purchased Sipco Molding Technologies of Meadville, adding another 65 employees. Later that year he acquired Multi-Tool Inc. and its subsidiaries, adding another 110 lucky employees to his roster. His charitable foundation is now in full swing, raising money for everything from community health initiatives to college scholarship funds.

To me Eric Hoover is the embodiment of the American dream, which by definition makes him a hero. In an industry that many pronounced dead in this country a long time ago, in a geography that has seen its share of rough economic times, this irrepressible force found opportunity in the most unlikely places and people.

Oh, by the way, Eric Hoover never went to college. He was too busy realizing real growth through an unwavering devotion to a worthy purpose.

Mix It Up!

Understand that Milkshake Moments most often occur when we are in a position to feel passionate about what we do. Growth leaders invest in other people's passions.

Chapter 23

Why People Work

I work with a lot of nonprofit associations. Recently I met a young man in his mid-20s, on his second real job out of school. He had wanted to put his all into a place with a purpose. He turned down a job offering more money to go with a national nonprofit health organization. He longed to be a part of a group making a real difference, so this fund-raising position was ideal. He came into the office his first day optimistic, enthusiastic, and ready to serve.

Unfortunately, things digressed quickly from Paul's expectations. The first day, he filled out paperwork. In week one, there was no training. His only instruction was a short talk about the two major events he needed to spearhead, with the dismissive instructions that "It's all there in the file cabinet."

Very soon Paul began to notice that nobody seemed to talk about the purpose of this huge national organization. He had thought he was signing up to help eradicate a disease that affects millions. Instead, all he ever heard about or discussed in meetings were budget figures, expense allocations, and office rules and procedures. He has trouble recalling the national director's name; the only time he hears anything from this executive's office is when there is a blast e-mail about some policy change. From the start he has felt untethered, unsupported, and uninformed, with nearly all pertinent information coming through the grapevine.

Agreeing to a lower salary than the other job offered is only the first financial hit Paul has taken. Because of a long-standing policy, reimbursable expenses are paid only monthly, no matter when they are submitted. So while he is laying out funds for event expenses such as balloons, ice, and snacks—in some months $600 to $800 worth—he gets reimbursed only when it is accounting's day to issue checks, not when his credit card bill is due. This new employee, earning less than $40,000 a year, essentially has to lend money to his giant employer each month.

As someone who sets up and runs charity events, Paul is seldom in the office. Yet he is not provided with a laptop (his boss thinks it's an unnecessary luxury), and there is no browser-based e-mail system. He must come into the office to check messages, even though the job has him out working in the field all day. What makes this even worse is that his predecessor gave a personal laptop

The Milkshake Moment

to the company as a charity donation. Paul can't use that one, though, because "It hasn't been approved by our IT department in D.C."

Despite the initial speed bumps, Paul was still ready to charge ahead. He buckled down and exceeded all previous records for donations in a major fund-raising event, bringing in several thousand dollars more than expected. He was ready for praise and a hearty slap on the back.

Instead, he found out in his evaluation that he was actually under the projected revenue budget for the year. It had been set artificially high several years before and never adjusted. "Oh, don't worry about that," the regional director told him. "That's just the way we budget around here. The other departments always make up for it."

Paul now better understands why he's the fourth person in four years to have his position. Meanwhile, his boss thinks they "just can't get good help these days," and the organization complains, "It's getting tougher each year to grow our level of donations and volunteers."

This enthusiastic, hardworking, goal-oriented employee came in as a star recruit that any organization would dream of hiring. Now he has one foot out the door—a door that could easily be propped open by the organization's 254-page employee handbook.

Let's contrast this true story and the organization's 254-page employee handbook with Nordstrom's. Yes, I know Nordstrom seems to get written up in half the business books out there, but according to *The Nordstrom Way* co-author Robert Spector, that company's handbook isn't even one full page. It just says this:

WELCOME TO NORDSTROM

We're glad to have you with our Company. Our number one goal is to provide outstanding customer service. Set both your personal and professional goals high. We have great confidence in your ability to achieve them.

Nordstrom Rules: Rule #1: Use your good judgment in all situations. There will be no additional rules.

Please feel free to ask your department manager, store manager, or division general manager any question at any time.

One of these organizations clearly demonstrates that it trusts you to do the right thing, and trusts you to ask for guidance when you're not sure how to best meet the overall objectives. The other organization hands you 254 pages of policies, procedures, and rules, most designed to thwart that tiny percentage of employees who can't be trusted. As a star employee or potential growth leader, where would you rather spend 40+ hours a week?

Work is about daily meaning as well as daily bread. For recognition as well as cash; for astonishment rather than torpor; in short, for a sort of life rather than a Monday through Friday sort of dying. We have a right to ask of work that it include meaning, recognition, astonishment, and life.

—Studs Terkel, *Working* (Pantheon Books, 1972)

It's really quite simple: Organizations ignore the reality of why people work at their own peril. By the way, Paul sent me his resume to distribute well before the end of his first year.

Mix It Up!

Recognize that people want to make a life, not just a living. When organizations honor individuals, Milkshake Moments become routine.

Extra Toppings

Recruit every day
Ask yourself, "Will winners want to work here? How do we create a culture, an environment, and a reputation that offers what people want in work?" Recruitment isn't a job opening; it's an organizational mind-set.

Train every day
Training should be a growth initiative, not a cost center. Growth leaders recognize the importance of training not just for new hires, but also for existing workers (which includes you, by the way). Leader, lead thyself.

149

Admit that you live in a seller's market

There are not enough good people to go around anymore. For skilled employees, this is a seller's market. The days when people were clamoring for an average job with minimal growth prospects are gone.

Handle employees like customers

Consider all that time and money your organization is putting into customer acquisition and retention. At some point, you'll need to similarly invest in employees to address the "people problem" problem. This is one obvious area in which you do have the ability to directly impact your organization's future chances for growth.

Section 6
Care for Customers

There are so many different kinds of organizations. Some serve customers. Some serve clients, while others serve patients, members, pupils, consumers, end users, citizens, policyholders, parishioners, donors, patrons, shoppers. I don't know what you call the people served by you and your organization, but I recognize that it matters.

If I start talking about customers to a room full of dentists, they mentally tune me out. They don't have customers; they have patients. I once used the word *distributors* with a group of computer hardware manufacturers and was later informed they called them *resellers*. Now, one of the first questions I ask any organization that I work with is, "What do you call those you serve?" Obviously I can't ask you, the reader, specifically what you call those you serve.

In the interest of semantic simplicity, I'm going to use the word *customer*. Please do your best to mentally insert your ideal term whenever the word *customer* appears.

I often ask leaders of organizations if they are truly customer driven. Are all the processes and procedures built into your organization there to better serve the customer? Invariably the answer is an emphatic "Yes!" Organizational leaders truly believe that they are highly customer driven.

And guess what? I believe them. I believe they are highly customer driven, because they wouldn't be in existence in today's competitive world if they weren't. Everyone says, "We love our customers." Put that phrase in Google and you'll get nearly 50,000 results. You'll get another 40,000 for "Our customers love us."

The modern organization exists to serve customers. We've all embraced that concept a long time ago. The problem is, it's becoming more difficult every day to differentiate on customer care.

One reason it has become harder to stand out from the pack is that almost all organizations have successfully prioritized the customer imperative. Seriously, think about it. Even the post office now works at customer satisfaction, as does my local Department of Motor Vehicles (while far from perfect, they are light-years ahead of where they were 10 years ago). I can get my movie tickets printed, my dry cleaning picked up, and my lunch delivered without ever leaving my computer. Everyone is offering a higher level of service than ever before.

It's also true to say that the better organizations get at meeting customer needs, the more our expectations rise. In effect, we've all become a bit spoiled. The truth is, our customers have never had it better, yet they feel less satisfied. Everyone wants everything faster, cheaper, and better than ever before, and feels perfectly justified in demanding it.

Care for Customers

It's tougher than ever out there, and even the best organizations struggle to simply keep up with their own reputations. That is why Milkshake Moments are so important for growth. No matter how customer-centric you believe your organization to be, there are always opportunities to better care for customers.

Chapter 24

Home Team Drops the Ball

Whoever is winning at the moment will always seem to be invincible.
—George Orwell, 1946 essay

As a teenager growing up in the north suburbs of Atlanta, my primary concerns were cars, sports, and the opposite sex (not necessarily in that order). Yet as my high school graduation day approached, it was hard not to notice the opening of two warehouselike retail stores. Long before there was a term *big box*, Home Depot pioneered a totally new way to sell home improvement supplies. Founders Bernie Marcus and Arthur Blank opened the two stores after being fired from a large chain of traditional hardware stores.

By the time I graduated from college, I knew more than a few people who had gone to work for Home Depot as store managers and were now millionaires because of the rising stock price. A few years later I found myself to be not only a loyal customer, but a preferred vendor as well. By this point the whole country had started to see orange.

155

Bernie and Arthur's original concept was brilliant. Offer the consumer the widest selection, the lowest price, and the best customer service. Everything the organization stood for revolved around its customers and their evolving needs. Even the organizational chart put store-level associates in the top position. The founders recognized that the secret to their success hinged on that personal connection to the customer.

By 2000, the chain had grown to over 1,000 stores and annual sales of $46 billion. In less than 20 years, Home Depot had become the nation's second-largest overall retailer. This meteoric climb can be directly attributed to an unwavering devotion to the cult of customer. But a meteor can't fly in a straight trajectory forever.

In December of 2000, the founders handed over the reins to an outsider. Robert Nardelli was a former lead dog at Jack Welch's General Electric. When Welch retired, Nardelli was passed over for the top slot and jumped ship to become CEO of the growing Home Depot chain. Wall Street analysts wondered how an executive without any retail experience was going to fare, but the economy was in its period of profitable "irrational exuberance" and Nardelli was widely assumed to be a quick study. What could possibly go wrong?

Almost from the beginning, I started to see differences. It began with fewer in-store associates. Later I noticed a little less product choice every visit. Checkout times seemed to steadily increase, too.

There was one specific change that was ultimately more damaging than any other. While the company will deny it to this day, it seemed to me that older, wiser experts were being edged out in favor of younger, less experienced shelf stockers. Home Depot helped popularize the phrase *do-it-yourself (DIY) home improvement.* I can't imagine that the original founders and leaders envisioned an entire do-it-yourself shopping experience. We were now forced to find our own product, drag it to checkout, scan the bulky items ourselves, and then lug it all back to our vehicle for loading. Eventually, it seemed as if the only orange apron in sight was sitting behind the contractors' desk—and I wasn't allowed to talk to them.

By 2005, the University of Michigan's annual American Customer Satisfaction Index showed Home Depot had slipped to dead last among all major U.S. retailers. In the name of cost efficiency (Nardelli came with a financial background), the once high-flying retailer now languished. Home Depot's stock was essentially flat for the six years when Bob Nardelli led the company, despite several share buybacks. At the same time, the stock price at chief competitor Lowe's jumped 230 percent during his reign.

Criticism of Nardelli rose among consumers, shareholders, and analysts alike. According to *USA Today*, he pulled out

157

an estimated $360 million in total compensation during his tenure. Meanwhile, shareholders were rewarded with a flat stock price and consumers with a flat shopping experience.

There's no doubt in my mind that the issues surrounding Home Depot were very complicated over the past few years. Was the chain overbuilt? Had it reached market saturation? What about international opportunities? Acquisitions? Wholesale markets? Rising interest rates? Yet I still can't imagine how anyone in Nardelli's position could lose sight of the one thing that allowed Home Depot to reinvent retail. At Home Depot the customer had always been king, and by the end of Nardelli's reign it appeared that the customer was held in contempt.

Anytime you see a hometown team grow to over 300,000 employees and win for so long, it's hard to watch a string of losing seasons. This should be a lesson to any organization: No matter how well you are doing, ignoring the needs of customers can weaken your organization faster than you can say "reversible ceiling fan."

Our favorite organizations regularly come to disappoint us. Nardelli's changes sacrificed what was most important to Home Depot's growth. In recent years, we've seen even the best stumble for the same reasons: Dell, the Federal Emergency Management Agency (FEMA), almost any big domestic U.S. airline. No organization, after exhibiting contempt for the customer, is immune from customer revolts.

Oh, by the way, Nardelli landed on his feet. Big Three automaker Chrysler hired him as their CEO the same year he got fired from Home Depot. If you drive a Dodge pickup or a Plymouth minivan, you might want to get a tune-up soon. Rumor has it that Nardelli's service dealers are simply going to hand you a wrench and a rag before too long.

Mix It Up!

Understand that your customers have more choices than ever before. Today, those you serve are about as flighty as a honeybee in a field full of wildflowers. Don't allow yourself to believe that your organization will always be the sweetest in the field.

Chapter 25

The Big Secret to Great Customer Service

We can assume that Home Depot leaders never consciously said, "I know, let's treat our customers like crap and see if we can put more money into our own pockets!" No, the bad customer service component of this story, and most like it, is merely symptomatic of a more fundamental failure.

So, here it is. The big secret to great customer service is that . . .

There *is* no big secret to great customer service.

Are there a few little secrets? Probably. We might even have already uncovered a few in earlier chapters. But if you've skipped straight to this chapter in search of an easy fix or a magic bullet, it's simply not that simple. Fully understanding the previous sections of this book should help you begin the arduous task of building a sustained growth organization. Never assume for a minute that it's going to be a straightforward or painless pursuit. By building a solid organizational foundation, true leaders are most able to put people in a position to deliver Milkshake Moments.

Store shelves are teeming with books on bad customer service and how to remedy it. Some are quite good. Some aren't. However, it seems to me, the idea that customers are important is pretty well ingrained in all of us. Being reminded that we should smile more and answer the phone with a can-do voice certainly doesn't hurt anything. Yet I maintain that when the best and brightest people are clear on the organization's purpose and are led by those they trust, good attitudes (and service) naturally follow.

We all learned with our lemonade stands as kids that "the customer is always right." That statement is mostly true. I don't need to list all the potential caveats here. The underlying sentiment behind this statement is still as valid today as it was 50 years ago. That is to say, as best we can, customers should be made to feel that our organization strives to fill their needs.

Yet when it comes to growth, customers are rarely right. Your customers cannot tell you how to grow your organization. Your customers can't even fully articulate what you can do to serve them better. I've sat in countless focus groups and seen endless surveys that point in one direction, only to watch customers move in exactly the opposite direction.

The Milkshake Moment

In the real estate industry I've often heard the saying "Buyers are liars." That is a pretty harsh sentiment, but not altogether untrue. They don't intend to lie. Usually they simply haven't had a chance to be honest with themselves yet. You ask any customer or potential customer a direct question, and they will give you the best answer they have at the moment. That doesn't mean it will have any relationship to what is ultimately right for them.

Yes, good customers should be made to feel that they are always right in a one-to-one customer service environment. Yet for you, the growth leader, it's crucial to understand this:

The customer isn't always right, but the customer is always human.

As hard as it can sometimes be to remember, customers are just people like you and me. And because they are human beings, they're not all the same. Trying to fill Joe's needs is different from trying to fill Susan's needs. They change their minds without even realizing it. They have bad days and take it out on us. They're fickle, they're busy, they're in a hurry, and they're focused on other things besides what you're focused on. You live your organization all the time. They experience your organization for a fleeting instant only when they really need you.

163

The Big Secret to Great Customer Service

Peter Drucker, the father of modern management, said over 50 years ago, "The purpose of business is to create and keep a customer." I'm sure he'd have no problem with me extending that sentiment to organizations as a whole. I don't intend for one instant to downplay the importance of the customer service function for any growth organization. My point is simply this: If we intend for our organization to be capable of Milkshake Moments, it will take much more than having everyone attend the *Who Moved My Customer's Chicken Soup?* seminar.

Mix It Up!

Reinforce the notion that customer loyalty isn't the responsibility of a department. Growth leaders build entire organizations that understand customers better than customers understand themselves.

Chapter 26

Even Geniuses Struggle to Serve

It is . . . our natural bent to recognize too late the
necessity for replenishing that which we exploit.
—William H. Whyte, *The Organization Man*
(Simon & Schuster, 1956), Chapter 16,
"The Fight against Genius"

There are plenty of organizations out there that appear to exist solely to infuriate us. Go ahead and send me an e-mail recounting your most ridiculous experience with a major airline, telecom carrier, credit card company, or cable provider (sourmilkshakes@stevenslittle.com).

Please feel free to include any stories regarding your fights with city hall. I'll even welcome diatribes railing against schools, hospitals, or that charity that won't quit calling your home at dinner time. Seriously, I feel your pain and I know it will make you feel better to get it off your chest. We both know that these types of organizations aren't really going to listen to you. I promise you I will.

It's easy to find fault with these customer-unfriendly organizations. Some are truly stupid, driven by pointless, muddled thinking. But most are mired in circumstances that would make even Albert Einstein scratch his bushy head. Twenty years ago we paid $1,000 for a round-trip coach class ticket that now costs $239, and yet we're less satisfied than ever before. A cell phone call that used to cost dollars now costs pennies, but we have trouble understanding why our costly technical questions are routinely routed from Topeka to Timbuktu. In my lifetime it has never been easier to submit payments to the Internal Revenue Service, but I never hear people speaking highly of the IRS's service level. Let's face it—in some ways these organizations have got it pretty tough, being forced to do more with less, only faster.

There's no need to recount endless stories about organizations that we all recognize are challenged in the service department. Truth be told, they fully recognize the problem too, spend an inordinate amount of time and money trying to rectify it, and still don't have it figured out. I maintain that there is actually much more we can learn about customer care—or lack thereof—from today's most admired organizations. Even the best routinely forget who really matters.

Take Apple, for example. It's hard to imagine an organization having more cachet with its customers than Apple. Yet I recently had an experience that flies in the face of all the glowing mythology surrounding the brand.

Visualizing vanilla milkshakes certainly gets me through my entire business travel day. However, the Apple iPod Shuffle has become my specific weapon against air travel tedium. This little $79 gizmo holds hundreds of my favorite songs. It's the only surefire remedy for screaming babies or multihour tarmac delays. You can imagine my grief when my nearly new Shuffle suddenly died on a flight to Las Vegas.

"No problem," said my sympathetic flight attendant. "There's an Apple store in the mall near your hotel. They can fix it there." I decided to make a store visit my first priority the next morning.

First impressions are important, and this store dazzled me. It was beautiful to look at: beautiful products, beautiful store layout, and crowded with beautiful people both working and playing. "How great is this?" I thought. I felt like I was entering the daytime version of a sleek nightclub.

I asked another patron how one goes about getting service and was directed to the get-a-number system located at what Apple calls the "genius bar" in the middle of the store. I got my number. The half hour wait went by quickly as I dove headfirst into the pool of in-store gadgetry.

"Number 57!" I heard someone call out from behind the bar. I raced over to the counter, anxious to bring the music back into my world.

Even Geniuses Struggle to Serve

My own personal genius was a smiling, bespectacled 20-something in a black T-shirt that read "Genius" just in case I was unclear about his qualifications. I explained my Shuffle dilemma and he responded, "Not a problem, sir—we'll have you taken care of in no time." While I waited for the ensuing hour-long diagnostic test to finish running, the thought occurred to me that our definitions of "in no time" apparently differed. I let Mr. Genius know that I was going to fetch a Cinnabon and an Orange Julius and would return directly.

Buzzing with both sugar and anticipation, I returned to hear the genius proclaim, "It's broken."

"Dazzling deduction, Boy Wonder," I thought but did not say.

A quick serial number check on my broken unit brought us both some welcome news. My Shuffle was still under warranty and he was authorized to simply give me a new one free of charge. It was not a perfect solution, given that I would have to reload the songs off my laptop, but I was genuinely impressed with the care. "Let me run to the back," Mr. Genius said, "and get you a replacement unit." We were now two hours into this experience, and I was about to become pretty darned satisfied.

Or maybe not. My now frowning genius reappeared from the back to inform me that they were temporarily out of replacement Shuffles. "Sir, can you come back tomorrow? We're expecting more replacement Shuffles tomorrow."

I directed his attention to the literally dozens of iPod Shuffles stacked approximately 10 feet to my left, in a rainbow of trendy colors. "Hey, here's a thought for you," I said with only the faintest hint of sarcasm. "Why don't we just crack open one of these boxes right here and I'll just shuffle right on out your door?"

Fifteen minutes later, Boy Wonder's boss, the Supreme Commander of all in-store geniuses, was still trying to help me understand how a replacement Shuffle's stock-keeping unit (SKU) was different from an in-store Shuffle's SKU. From what my pea brain could gather, they were authorized to give me only the former and not the latter. It was now beginning to cross my mind that these self-proclaimed geniuses might not be quite as swift as their shirts would have us believe.

They had a full stack of Shuffles, half of my morning, and a valid serial number, but they still couldn't deliver an iShake. Needless to say, I returned to my hotel a bit iRate. (Sorry, that's my last iPun—iPromise.)

By any measure, Apple's entrée into the retail sector has been a monumental success. Three years after opening its first outlet, Apple Stores reached $1 billion in revenue, faster than any retailer in history. Today sales

Even Geniuses Struggle to Serve

exceed $1 billion a quarter. According to a 2007 report by industry analyst Sanford C. Bernstein, Apple's retail the sales are an astounding $4,032 per square foot, four times retail sales of Best Buy, the next-highest consumer electronics retailer. The monumental success of its retail concept helped Apple attain a top 10 position within *Fortune* magazine's list of most admired companies. Literally no one does it better than Apple.

Delivering great customer service isn't about getting it right every time. Instead, it's about getting it right more often—more often than your competitors, more often than it is expected, more often than you did before. Apple, with no experience in retail, has clearly gotten it right more often than anyone, from store design to hiring to product offerings. Apple in many ways has revolutionized what's possible with an in-store shopping experience.

So the question becomes: Was this one bad experience in early 2007 an inconsequential lapse or a more important sign that the Apple tree is beginning to bend under the weight of its own growth? Obviously, the more stores that Apple opens, the more experiences customers will have, both good and bad. Maybe it meant nothing.

By the summer of 2007, I couldn't help but notice the consumer backlash following the incredibly successful introduction of the Apple iPhone. Customer dissatisfaction ranged from inadequate stock to a confusing pricing strategy to buggy software updates that turned many iPhones into what industry analysts began to call "iBricks." "We need to do a better job taking care of our early iPhone customers as we aggressively go after new ones," said Apple founder and CEO Steve Jobs in an open letter that fall on the company web site. "Our early customers trusted us, and we must live up to that trust with our actions."

If the uniquely successful geniuses at Apple are capable of losing customer focus, where does that leave the rest of us morons?

For the twenty-first-century organization, yesterdays don't matter. Home Depot has come to learn that the hard way. The Starbucks brand is an international juggernaut, but even the founder and chairman has recently admitted that the "Starbucks experience" has suffered with its rapid expansion. After losing sight of the importance of trust, even venerable institutions like the American Red Cross and the Catholic Church have managed to squander generations of goodwill.

Where were the true leaders when these organizations started to lose their way? At the first sign of trouble, would you have been the organizational hero who steps up to say, "Folks, we have a problem here that requires our immediate attention and action"?

Even Geniuses Struggle to Serve

Throughout this book, I've stressed that managers simply managing won't foster growth. It takes leadership. Once the growth takes hold, it takes a hero to triumph over the new and seemingly impossible challenges all growth organizations inevitably will face. Ultimately, your customers require heroes who take a stand and devote themselves to anticipating and filling their future needs. If you don't consider yourself to have hero potential, remember that none of the heroes we've met in this book think of themselves as being anything special, either. In their minds, they're just doing the right thing.

Mix It Up!

Consider that doing the right thing is almost always harder in practice than in theory. Milkshake Moments are delivered by everyday heroes who stand up and make a difference.

Chapter 27

It Takes a Hero

Another hero of mine was born in 1908, in a mining camp in northern Alabama. His parents had immigrated to the United States from Scotland, and young Tom was the fourth of an eventual clan of nine. The family moved around quite a bit during Tom's childhood, living in Alabama and Illinois before eventually settling in southern Indiana. Like his father and brothers before him, he quit going to school at the age of 14 to join the men in his family deep below the earth's surface.

He regularly worked 12-hour days and 60-hour weeks. The job was both tortuous and dangerous. Although he was never caught in an explosion, his brothers bore the tell-tale scars of blasting accidents. When the mines began to be tapped out and work became less reliable, a workers' strike followed. Young Tom left the mines one day at the age of 18 and vowed to himself that he would never return. To that end he went back to his studies and earned a high school degree.

Luckily for Tom, he also had a gift to fall back on. Legend has it he could pitch back-to-back nine-inning games of baseball without losing any zip on his slider. His athletic prowess eventually earned him a full scholarship to a small teachers college in Terre Haute, Indiana (now called Indiana State University). He was the first person in his family ever to go to college.

There Tom excelled in four sports, running track and playing baseball in the same season. He would pitch an inning, run over to the track to compete in the high hurdlers, and then head back to pitch the bottom of the next inning.

After graduation, Tom and his young wife became teachers. By 1937 he was teaching biology and coaching football in the capital city of Indianapolis. In 1959 he became principal of a large high school in the city—not bad for a kid who dropped out of school in the eighth grade.

Today a portrait of Tom resides in the auditorium that now bears his name at Howe High School in Indianapolis. As a coach, a teacher, and an administrator, Thomas Stirling was a hero to the community he served.

For me, he was a hero because he was my Paw-Paw, my mother's father, and a walking, talking personification of the American dream. He left us about 10 years ago and he is greatly missed.

My hero Paw-Paw had his own hero, a man named John Wooden. As coaches, teachers, and fellow alumni of that small school in Terre Haute, these two Hoosiers came to know one another. As a child, watching UCLA dominate the game I loved most, I can still remember my grandfather pointing to the screen and saying, "There is the man you want to be like."

When I asked Coach Wooden if he remembered my grandfather, he said, "Oh, yes, I remember Tom. I remember Eva, too." (I guess my grandma was "a looker.")

After graduating from Purdue University, John Wooden also went on to earn a teaching degree from what is now Indiana State University. Upon returning from World War II, Wooden accepted the position of both athletic director and head basketball coach at the school. Coach Wooden led the scrappy Sycamore hoopsters to a conference title in 1947 and an invitation to the National Association of Intercollegiate Basketball tournament being held in Kansas City—a precursor to today's National Collegiate Athletic Association (NCAA) championship.

At that time, the tournament had a pointless policy banning African-American players from competing. Wooden refused the invitation. If you wanted Wooden's team, you had to accept the whole team. The Sycamores had one African-American player, and Wooden would never have left one member of his team behind. I'll bet the young coach took plenty of hits from both alumni and fans for turning down such a prestigious invitation for the fledgling program.

Obviously, looking back now, it was the right thing to do, but it must have been hard for others to see that at the time. Coach Wooden was guided by a clear moral compass that could never be swayed by popular opinion. "Be more concerned with your character than your reputation," he once said. "Your character is what you really are, while your reputation is merely what others think you are."

Remember in Chapter 11 I told you that Coach Wooden left me with two lessons I'd never forget? The first thing he said was this: "I never set out to win championships. I always knew that I wanted to help young people achieve beyond their own expectations of themselves. Championships were a by-product of that effort." But it was his second lesson that I've saved until now. It's his second lesson that truly resonated with me. It's amazing when your heroes live up to your highest expectations.

During the height of the civil rights unrest of the 1960s, when Los Angeles was literally on fire with racial tension, Wooden overheard a reporter ask one of his African-American players, "Can you tell me about the racial problems on the team?"

The Milkshake Moment

The player replied, "You don't know our coach, do you? He doesn't see race at all—he just sees ballplayers." The young man turned and walked away, effectively ending the interview. My hero told that story to over a thousand people in Los Angeles. He ended by saying, "I was proud that day." After he spoke, Coach Wooden told me, "If that's all I'm ever remembered for, I'd be okay with that."

I have an opinion. My opinion doesn't necessarily reflect that of my publisher, my editor, or my family. It's just my opinion, and I encourage you to take it for what it is worth.

I believe that we live in a great nation. Five hundred years from now or a thousand years from now, I don't think we'll be remembered for capitalism or democracy. What we will be remembered for is being the first group of human beings to write a purpose-driven plan that included the words, "All men are created equal."

I'm a political agnostic and an organizational growth realist. I would be remiss if I didn't share with you some numbers that I think truly matter. When this great nation was founded, half the world looked like me—Caucasian— and half the world did not. Today, 80 percent of the world doesn't look like me anymore. Forty percent of the United States doesn't look like me anymore.

I suggest that you try to have a 20/20 vision of the year 2050. I don't know if you'll still be around by then. I know in 2050 I'll be exactly Coach Wooden's age when I met him. I recently heard a futurist predict that by 2050, only 4 percent of the world's population will look like me.

In my mind, for true leaders interested in growth, it's imperative that we do everything in our power to better understand one another. We must learn how to work with people who don't look like us, don't think like us, and don't talk like us. In my opinion, race is the defining issue of our time.

My opinion is not a social or political commentary. Rather, it's simply logic based on demographic shifts that show no signs of altering their course.

(You can't expect the unexpected, but you can master the obvious forces of change.)

To me, the need to better understand giant fundamental shifts is as obvious as a milkshake.

Mix It Up!

Take a stand. Sustainable growth doesn't often follow the path of least resistance. It is hard to find a hero who hasn't, at one time or another, taken an unpopular position.

178

Chapter 28

The Future Is Already Here . . . Some Folks Just Aren't Getting the Memos

In order to consistently deliver Milkshake Moments, it is essential that you regularly take the time to step back and examine the obvious forces of change shaping the world.

As we discussed earlier, modern man has been on this planet for roughly 200,000 years, and for 99.9 percent of that time, we were pretty much the same. Yet somehow, in just the past 100 years, everything about the human condition has changed. The shifts in where we live, how we live, and who we live with affect literally everything, including organizations. Who you hire, who you buy from, and who you serve have rapidly evolved and will continue to change for the rest of your life.

The year 1900 was pivotal in the history of mankind. In 1900, only 12 percent of the world's population lived in a city of more than a million people. By 1960, one-third

179

of the world's population lived in a city of over a million. Today it's nearly half. By 2028, two-thirds of the world's population will be living in a city of more than a million people. We never lived in cities for approximately 200,000 years, but somehow the vast majority of the world will reside in a metropolitan area very soon.

In 1900, the life expectancy of the average boy born in the United States was under 50 years. Today, experts predict that the average American girl born this year will have a life expectancy of over 100.

Much has been made of the general aging of the population in the United States. But this "grayification" isn't happening only here—the trend is actually more pronounced in Japan and Western Europe. With advances in technology and medicine, it's not unrealistic to believe that many 40-year-olds today will live another 100 years.

Sixteen percent of the current U.S. population speaks Spanish as their first language. Chances are high that this number will exceed 20 percent in your organization's lifetime. More people live in just China and India today than lived in the entire world in 1950. Demographic shifts like these affect all organizations.

We live in a time when scientists can cross an orb weaver spider with a Nigerian dwarf goat and cobble together a bulletproof vest from the weblike proteins floating within the goat's milk. A woman in Texas spent $50,000 to clone her dead kitty-cat "Nicky." The world's first cloned cat had kittens (conceived the old-fashioned way) last year. As of January 2008, glow-in-the-dark pigs have been successfully bred in Taiwan.

Biofuels appear poised to offer a real solution to shortages of fossil fuels. Americans tend to see genetically modified foods as a potential source of efficient sustenance for the world. Europeans call this "frankenfood" and fear it will create food-chain chaos. Either way, changes in biological science will have a tremendous impact on us all.

And when it comes to the future of technology in an information age, I agree with Andy Grove, co-founder of Silicon Valley chipmaker Intel. When asked about the future of technology, he told *BusinessWeek* magazine that "we can't even glimpse the potential."

Increasingly, getting your organization to another level will be about learning how to take advantage of these obvious evolutions that lead to eventual revolutions. While much of the future may lie beyond your immediate view, it is crucial that you take the time to regularly consider the impact that these macro forces of change will have on you and your organization. No one can predict the future, but twenty-first-century growth leaders are better able to see the future of their opportunity.

181

The Future Is Already Here . . .

Mix It Up!

Anticipate the world's changing needs. Therein lies the key to future Milkshake Moments.

Extra Toppings

Monitor ongoing changes

A twenty-first-century growth leader is like a futurist. Once a big new thing hits your newsletters, trade publications, or the popular media, it is too late for you to capitalize on it. Look for the ripples of change on the periphery of your field of vision.

Consider the potential impacts of these changes

Tsunamis begin as ripples. Through experience and wisdom, a leader can distinguish between the ripples that become giant waves of change and the inconsequential ripples that create only a small splash.

Develop a response

Once you have identified the next big wave, the question becomes, how will you choose to ride it? Growth leaders spend the majority of their time, money, and effort on the opportunities of tomorrow.

Make more milkshakes

I mean this literally. While useful as an analogy, the milk-shake is also a delicious beverage treat. I encourage you to enjoy one on a regular basis. Indulging in life's simple pleasures can make getting out of bed a lot more fun.

Index

193

Supervisory roles, 55
Sustainable growth, 21,
  24, 178
Swingline, 51

T

Technology, future of, 181
Tension, energy and,
  28–29
Terkel, Studs, 149
Theywontletus virus, 88
Thinking:
  information age
    and, 63
  organizational, 28
  positive, 33
  rational, 45
Timely attribute, growth
  leaders and, 32–33, 116
Toyota, 102
TPS report, 51
Trade associations, growth
  for, 20
Training, growth and, 149
Transparent attribute,
  growth leaders and,
  35–36
Travels for business, 3–7

Trust:
  authenticity and, 31–37
  losing, 171
  in teams, 118, 127
Twentieth century:
  organizations in, 15, 27
  world's population in,
    179–180
Twenty-first century:
  growth leaders, 182
  organizations in, 171
  world's population in, 180
2001: A Space Odyssey
  (Movie), 51–52

U

U. S. Bureau of Labor
  Statistics, 133, 134
*U. S. News & World
  Report,* 97
U. S. population, 180
Udell, Howard R., 80
Underperformers, organiza-
  tions and, 104
United States, economy of,
  85–88
University of Michigan's
  Annual American